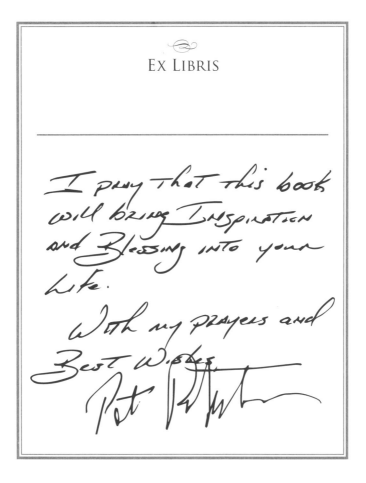

EX LIBRIS

_I pray that this book
will bring Inspiration
and Blessing into your
Life._

_With my prayers and
Best Wishes,_

Pat Robertson

THE POWER OF THE HOLY SPIRIT IN YOU

PAT ROBERTSON

THE POWER
of the
HOLY SPIRIT
in You
Understanding *the* Miraculous
Power of God

SALEM
BOOKS

an imprint of Regnery Publishing
Washington, D.C.

Scripture quotations marked AMP are taken from the Amplified® Bible. Copyright © 1954, 1958, 1962, 1964, 1965, 1987 by The Lockman Foundation. Used by permission. www.lockman.org.

Scripture quotations marked AMPC are taken from the Amplified® Bible. Copyright © 1954, 1958, 1962, 1964, 1965, 1987 by The Lockman Foundation. Used by permission. www.lockman.org.

Scripture quotations marked KJV are taken from the King James Version, public domain.

Scripture quotations marked MEV are taken from the Modern English Version. Copyright © 2014 by Military Bible Association. Used by permission. All rights reserved.

Scripture quotations marked NASB are taken from the (NASB®) New American Standard Bible®. Copyright © 1960, 1971, 1977, 1995, and 2020 by The Lockman Foundation. Used by permission. All rights reserved. www.lockman.org.

Scriptures marked NET are taken from the Bible® http://netbible.com. Copyright ©1996, 2019. Used with permission from Biblical Studies Press, L.L.C. All rights reserved.

Scripture quotations marked NIV are taken from the Holy Bible, New International Version®, NIV®. Copyright © 1973, 1978, 1984, 2011 by Biblica, Inc.® Used by permission of Zondervan. All rights reserved worldwide. www.zondervan.com. The "NIV" and "New International Version" are trademarks registered in the United States Patent and Trademark Office by Biblica, Inc.®

Scripture quotations marked NKJV are taken from the New King James Version®. Copyright © 1982 by Thomas Nelson. Used by permission. All rights reserved.

Scriptures marked NLT are taken from the Holy Bible, New Living Translation. Copyright © 1996, 2004, 2015 by Tyndale House Foundation. Used by permission of Tyndale House Ministries, Carol Stream, Illinois 60188. All rights reserved.

Scriptures marked WEB are taken from The Word English Bible, public domain.

Salem Books™ is a trademark of Salem Communications Holding Corporation.
Regnery® is a registered trademark and its colophon is a trademark of Salem Communications Holding Corporation.

ISBN: 978-1-68451-251-5
eISBN: 978-1-68451-256-0

Library of Congress Control Number: 2021946352

Published in the United States by Salem Books, An Imprint of Regnery Publishing
A Division of Salem Media Group, Washington, D.C., www.SalemBooks.com

Manufactured in the United States of America

10 9 8 7 6 5 4 3 2 1

Books are available in quantity for promotional or premium use. For information on discounts and terms, please visit our website: www.SalemBooks.com.

CONTENTS

BEGINNING ix

OLD COVENANT 19

NEW COVENANT 91

BEGINNING

ONE GOD, OR THREE

In the Book of Genesis, the first chapter of the Bible, we read these words: "In the beginning God (prepared, formed, fashioned, and) created the heavens and the earth. The earth was without form and an empty waste, and darkness was upon the face of the very great deep. The Spirit of God was moving (hovering, brooding) over the face of the waters" (Genesis 1:1–2, AMPC). So, in the beginning of time, before the earth had been formed, not only was Elohim (God) present, but also someone called in Hebrew *Ruach Elohim* (the Spirit of God). Then, Scripture tells us that the Spirit of God was brooding over the waters. The image here is of a mother hen covering her babies. It is safe to say that the Spirit of God was present at the very creation of the world, and that the Spirit of God is distinct from God the Father. Otherwise, why would it be necessary to speak of God as one being and the Spirit of God as another being?

But then something else is revealed. "And God said, 'Let there be light, and there was light'" (Genesis 1:3). So a third factor is introduced to us: the Word of God. In the first chapter of the first book of the Bible, we see God, the Spirit of God, and the Word of God. We will learn later that Jesus Christ is known as the Word of God. There are three distinct beings: God, the Spirit of God, and the Word of God.

The Gospel of John gives us further understanding about the second person of the Godhead, the Word. John's gospel says, "In the beginning was the Word, and the Word was with God, and the Word was God. He was with God in the beginning. Through him all things were made; without him nothing was made that has been made" (John 1:1–3 NIV). The Greek preposition *dia* is used at this point and can be translated as "by" or "through." However, three of the best translations translate it as "through," and therefore, for the purposes of this manuscript, I will be using the translation of *dia* as "through." The Creative Mind (the Father) expressed Himself through the Word (the Son), but the active power to effectuate the Father's command comes by the Spirit of God.

What do we learn from this biblical beginning? Father God appears as the creative mind, and He expresses Himself with His word. Would that not be adequate to achieve what is necessary? Apparently not. I don't want to read too much into the early narrative, but it does seem that the effective power to activate God's will and spoken word throughout His creation comes through the Spirit of God.

This book is about the Holy Spirit, and throughout the Bible, the Holy Spirit is the power which activates the will of God and the Word of God throughout His creation, and certainly to those of us made in His image.

We can fast-forward now to the beginning of the ministry of Jesus Christ when, as a young man of thirty, He submitted Himself to the ritual of baptism at the hand of a fiery preacher known as John the Baptist. At that moment, Scripture tells us that a dove (the symbol of the Holy Spirit) descended from Heaven and sat upon Jesus, and a voice from Heaven—the voice of God the Father—said, "This is my beloved Son, in whom I am well pleased" (Matthew 3:17 NKJV). Here again is the Trinity of God—Father, Son, and Holy Spirit—the Father, the creative mind of the Trinity; the Son, the expression of God or the Word of God; and the Holy Spirit, the activating power of God throughout His creation.

We have learned that God the Father is God, God the Son is God, and God the Holy Spirit is also God. And yet together, they are one.

People have laughed at this concept, have been confused by it, and have brought forth heresy to explain it. The Islamic faith, in fact, refers to Christians as polytheists, which to its adherents is a gross error. They say, "We serve one god, who is Allah." I wonder who Allah is. The flags of Algeria, Libya, Turkey, and Pakistan, for example, have the crescent moon on them. For a time, I considered the possibility that Hubal, the Moon God of Mecca, was indeed the Allah that is worshipped by the Islamic people. However, the weight of scholarship swings in another direction. Was Allah a derivation of an Arabic term much like the Hebrew *El*, or did it partake of the Phoenician name for *lord*, which was *Baal*? The best scholarship I have been able to find indicates that Allah is in truth a derivation of Baal. Whatever the origin of Allah, I want to say emphatically that Christians and Jews do not worship Allah, but the Covenant God of the Hebrews who is identified by the tetragrammaton *YHWH*...or *YAHWEH*.

Do Christians really serve three Gods? The answer is no: we serve one God eternally existent in three persons—God the Father, God the Son, and God the Holy Spirit.

Some thinkers, in trying to rationalize this concept, have used the analogy of water. Water is a liquid. When heated it becomes steam. When frozen it can become ice. They say this explains how there can be three in one. Regrettably, that explanation leads to a heresy known as Modalistic Monarchianism. In this explanation, water turns into steam, or water turns into ice. But that's not what happens to the Trinity of God. The Father remains the Father, and yet He is God. The Son remains the Son, and yet He is God. The Holy Spirit remains the Holy Spirit, and yet He is still God. Three in one.

Perhaps a better explanation of the Trinity would be to run a light through a prism and see the light break down into the component parts of red, green, and blue.

No, as Christians we don't serve three Gods; we serve one God. As the so-called *Shema* (found in Deuteronomy 6:4) proclaims, "Hear, O Israel: the LORD [YHWH] our God, the LORD [YHWH] is one" (NIV). One Lord is eternally existent in three beings—Father, Son, and Holy Spirit.

Jesus said on the eve of His departure, "If I go away, I will send to you another comforter, whom the world cannot receive. He will take of mine and reveal it unto you" (John 14:16–17

KJV). Yet John 14:26 tells us, "But the advocate, the Holy Spirit, whom the Father will send in my name, will teach you all things and will remind you of everything I have said to you" (NIV).

We are also told that the Father will send the Holy Spirit. Out of this has arisen a debate as to whether the Holy Spirit proceeds from the Son or from the Father. It seems to me that the Bible assures us that both the Father and His Son want the Holy Spirit to come into the lives of His people to reveal truth and to strengthen them.

In the original language of the Bible, the word *comforter* does not mean a soft, cuddly quilt. The two parts of that word are *con*, which means "with," and *fort*, which means "strength." The Holy Spirit will be sent to believers to bring strength to them; then to reveal to them truth about Jesus, His nature, and His mission on Earth. In addition, the Holy Spirit will reveal to us the nature of the Father and His will on Earth.

Think what this means for a person's prayer life. He or she is to pray to the Father; in the name of the Son, Jesus Christ; and in the power of the Holy Spirit.

It is now time for us to examine how the Holy Spirit brings blessings and instructions to God's people.

CHAPTER 2

MOSES'S VEIL

When we come to the writings of the Apostle Paul in his second letter to the church at Corinth, we find a remarkable juxtaposition between the Old Covenant personified by Moses and Joshua and the New Covenant personified by Christian believers filled with the Holy Spirit.

Paul reminds us that when Moses ascended Mount Sinai to meet forty days and forty nights with YHWH, his face took on the brightness of an angelic being. In fact, his face reflected the glory of YHWH so brightly that he needed to wear a veil to dim the glow. Paul then says that "if the ministry that brought condemnation was glorious, how much more glorious is the ministry that brings righteousness!" (2 Corinthians 3:9 NIV).

Paul laments the fact that when the message of the law of Moses was read to his fellow Hebrews, it was obscured by what appeared to be a veil. And until that veil was lifted, his fellow Israelites remained ignorant of the true power of God. But if the veil was lifted through the working of the Holy Spirit, it became to those Hebrews like life from the dead.

The English word Lord is actually a poor translation for the Hebrew word YHWH. Yet in the New Testament, Jesus Christ is referred to as "the Lord" or "the Lord Almighty." The English word Lord used by the Apostle Paul in 1 Corinthians is a translation of the Greek word *kurios*, which essentially has the meaning of "master" or "leader." This Greek word is used hundreds of times in the New Testament as a term of honor for Jesus. For instance, in Mark 1:3 we read, "Prepare ye the way of the Lord" (KVJ). In Mark 2:28 Jesus said, "The Son of Man is also Lord of the Sabbath" (NKJV). In Mark 9:24 the hurting man said, "Lord, I believe, help thou mine unbelief" (KJV). And in Matthew, when speaking of the judgment of the Gentile nations after His return, Jesus described those who showed mercy to His brothers. They said to Him, "Lord, when did we see you hungry and thirsty or sick and in prison?" In short, in reference to Himself Jesus used the term *kurios*. And in His interactions with many, many people all over Palestine, He was called "*kurios*" or "Lord" (or occasionally "Rabbi") by those who saw Him.

You can imagine my amazement when I read that the Apostle Paul said, "Now the Lord is the Spirit, and where the Spirit of the Lord is there is freedom" (2 Corinthians 3:17 NIV).

The Apostle Paul was saying that the ministry of the Holy Spirit was much more glorious than the ministry of the covenant given to Israel by Moses. For to him the law did not bring life, but spiritual stultification; whereas the Holy Spirit brought forth a more glorious covenant—and with it, freedom.

In fact, it's more than just freedom. Paul goes on to say, "And we all, who with unveiled faces contemplate the Lord's glory, are being transformed into his image with ever-increasing glory, which comes from the Lord, who is the Spirit" (2 Corinthians 3:18 NIV). The Apostle Paul is clearly saying that the Holy Spirit creates the character of Jesus Christ in the believer. According to him, those who believe in Jesus Christ take on the very nature of Jesus because of the work of the Holy Spirit.

Paul says the Lord (*kurios*) is the *pneuma hagios* (Greek translations: *pneuma* = "spirit"; *hagios* = "holy"). Frankly, this is an astounding statement to me. We have already seen that according to the Scriptures, Jesus promised His disciples that if He went away, He would send the Comforter to them. In other places of the gospels, we are told that Jesus and the Father send the Holy Spirit to the believers. Those statements preserve intact our concept of the Holy Trinity: Father, Son, and Holy Spirit. But what happens to our understanding of the Trinity if the Son of God *is* the Spirit? Are the Son of God and the Holy Spirit so close in the Trinity that there needs to be no distinction between Them? If the Holy Spirit creates Jesus's character in believers, does this remove the separate identities so that Paul can say "the Lord is the Spirit?" Not really. Paul was clearly Trinitarian, and so am I.

Perhaps we had better leave the theological speculation to those who spend their lifetime pondering the mysteries of the Bible. For the everyday Christian, the good news is that the Holy Spirit will cause you to think like Jesus, to act like Jesus, and to demonstrate the power of Jesus. What an absolutely glorious prospect for all of us who live under the New Covenant that the Lord has brought upon the earth.

Again, I repeat the words of the Apostle Paul (2 Corinthians 3:18): "And we all, who with unveiled faces contemplate the Lord's glory, are being transformed into his image with ever-increasing glory, which comes from the Lord, who is the Spirit" (NIV).

CHAPTER 3

THE ANGEL OF LIGHT

The understanding we now have of the Holy Spirit came to us through the ministry of Jesus Christ while He was here on Earth and after He ascended into Heaven. Nevertheless, God did work in Israel through prophets and holy men of God who were moved by the Spirit. We want now to consider the instances in the Old Testament, when God's Spirit was at work among His servants.

Genesis tells us in seven instances, "And God said...." Through those declarations, God prepared the earth. It may have taken several million years for all of them to be accomplished, but in the process, there was a planet at just the right distance from the sun to bring warmth and photosynthesis to growing plants. There was precisely the proper mixture of carbon and hydrogen and other essential gases for life. There was a magnetic core which kept the atmosphere surrounding the earth. There was a moon that regulated the spinning of the planet through the heavens. There was soil for vegetables and seeds for trees that bear fruit, along with cedar, cypress, oak, and walnut trees, which provided the necessary lumber for mankind to build structures, such as the one found hundreds of years later in God's command to Noah to build an ark of wood. There was coal and iron for mankind's building projects in the future. There were even rare-earth elements, which have in our day become so vital for computers and other electronics. There was an ocean filled with fish, and on the land there were animals to provide meat and clothing for mankind. And God placed this little planet in a solar system as part of the Milky Way Galaxy, nestled safely in a quiet part of the universe.

I read those first chapters in the Book of Genesis as the preparation for God's eighth act of recorded creation: the introduction of the human race. At this point in the narrative, the emphasis shifts from God the Creative Mind's speaking to the Son to the Holy Spirit's actually creating and forming a universe.

Then, as the eighth act of creation, we read a plural: "Let us make mankind in our image, in our likeness, so that they may rule over the fish in the sea, the birds in the sky, over the livestock, and all the wild animals that move along the ground" (Genesis 1:26 NIV). Some people have said the use of the words *we* and *our* is simply the plural of *majesty*, as a king would say, "We are pleased with our subjects." I don't agree with this interpretation. I think we had a conference of the Father, the Son, and the Holy Spirit decreeing the creation of the unique being who was to be put in charge of this marvelous creation which the Trinity of God had brought into being through millions of years.

What then was the image of God—the so-called *Imago Dei*? I used to think that Imago Dei was a mirror that reflected the glory of God, which through sin had been shattered so the glory was no longer clearly seen. I believe an understanding of the Trinity leads us to a more robust conclusion. If the Trinity made mankind in Its image, then each human should reflect, in some way, the characteristics of each member. If this is true, think what it means for each one of us. We have the ability to conceive amazing things! In truth, throughout history mankind has brought forth incredible feats of creative genius which, in my opinion, only scratch the tip of the iceberg of the capability placed in us. As creatures made in God's image, we have the ability to speak the Word and see it come to pass. Jesus told His disciples that if they had faith as small as a tiny grain of mustard seed, they could say to the Mount of Olives that it must remove itself and fall into the Dead Sea, and it would obey them. Through the power of the Holy Spirit, nothing would be impossible for us. That is the true *Imago Dei*. We, as human beings redeemed by Jesus Christ, have the power on Earth to take benign dominion over this marvelous planet, which a gracious God has placed in our hands. This is why the fall of man is so extraordinarily tragic. To this day, we see human beings made in the image of God prostrate themselves before alcohol, cocaine, heroin, marijuana, and tobacco, which are themselves products of the plants and vegetables God commissioned man to rule over. Our minds cannot conceive how glorious a future we would have enjoyed had Adam and his descendants obeyed God.

We are told that God placed the first human beings in a garden of delights. They had everything necessary to satisfy their minds and their senses. They only needed to reach out their hands to taste delicious fruits. C. S. Lewis described that fruit in one of his fictional books as so delicious that men at a later age would have killed for just a taste. The fields were covered with gloriously colored flowers. The trees were in vivid bloom and the sky was filled with birds of glorious plumage. The first man, Adam, was in a state of complete innocence. To be complete, he needed to learn the difference between right and wrong. To accomplish this, God placed a tree in the garden called the Tree of the Knowledge of Good and Evil. God told Adam he could eat any fruit in the garden. There was no law or regulation whatsoever, so sin would have been impossible, because without law there is no sin. Can you imagine how wonderful it would be to live in a society where there are absolutely no rules except the law of love? In God's perfect universe there was no hatred, no bitterness, no killing, no sickness, no disease. All the universe reflected the glory and splendor of the Great Creator.

In the early Genesis account, there is no discussion of the creation of another race of beings that we know as angels. These beings were spiritual messengers formed to heed God's commands. The angels lived in the absolute presence of Almighty God and knew His splendor firsthand. They were divided into various categories according to their power. Among them was a group known as archangels, but the most powerful of all of the angels was known as Lucifer (or the "Light One"). Lucifer belonged to a class of angels known as *cherubim*, whose exalted task was to cover the very holiness of God. In later scriptures he was referred to as the covering angel. Lucifer was magnificent in his splendor, radiated beauty, was enormously powerful, and had access to the Creator, which gave him privileges no other created being possessed.

The tragedy for Lucifer came when he had occasion to behold his own beauty. Soon after, he began to contemplate his own wisdom. Then his exalted mind filled with plans for the government of the universe, which Lucifer felt were superior to those of the Creator. How long did this take? One year of our time? Ten? One hundred thousand years? One million years? We don't know how long it took, but we do know it happened. The first sin was pride on behalf of a creature who said very simply, "My way is better than God's way."

As we look throughout the history of mankind at the ravings of powerful dictators, the writings of the philosophers, and the discussions of the thinkers, invariably they boil down to one simple truth: "I did it my way, and my way is better than God's way."

So consumed with pride in his own beauty, Lucifer launched a rebellion against Almighty God. According to the Book of Revelation in the Bible, he took one-third of the angels with him, and as punishment for his rebellion he was cast down to Earth along with what are called the "fallen angels." Many people have wondered why an all-powerful God did not merely use His power to destroy this vicious enemy and rid the universe of him. The answer is clear if you think about it: If God used His power to destroy His enemies—if He caused blasphemers' tongues to rot in their mouths as the words of blasphemy were uttered—then no creature would serve Him voluntarily in love. They would serve Him because of fear.

In human terms, a father wants his little son to run to him, throw his arms around him, and yell, "Daddy, you're home! I love you!" What type of father would want a child who cowered at his presence and respected him only because of the fear of punishment? God's plan involved a contest to show that love will triumph, that a human being would love Him so much that he would die in obedience to Him and, therefore, set an example for the rest of creation. This is the cosmic struggle set in motion by the rebellion of Satan.

However, there is much more in our narrative that deals with the Holy Spirit and fallen humanity before God's ultimate triumph in the death and resurrection of the Son of God. After Satan fell, we find that he entered into a serpent that was one of the creatures in the garden. He saw an opportunity to bring Adam's wife, Eve, into sin.

As Eve was walking in the Garden of Eden, the serpent spoke to her and said (in my paraphrase), "Are you aware that God is keeping something good from you?" Eve's curiosity was aroused as the serpent went on to say, "He is withholding from you a fruit that will make you as wise as God." Eve replied, "We are commanded not to eat the fruit. We are not even supposed to touch it." At that, Satan knew that he had her, because she added to the Word of God by making it more difficult.

As an aside, I would use that as a cautionary tale to my reader. Even Jesus Christ Himself did not play mind games with Satan. Jesus was well aware that Satan was a liar and the father of lies. To engage Satan in a philosophical debate would have involved Jesus's fighting through a web of lies. Jesus, who the Bible tells us was filled with the Holy Spirit, declared over and over again the simple Word of God. To each temptation of Satan, Jesus merely said, "It is written" (Luke

4:8 NIV). Then, He set forth in simple terms the clear Word of biblical truth.

But Eve had neither the wisdom nor the biblical knowledge that Jesus Christ enjoyed. She believed the devil's lie and reached out her hand, took the fruit, and ate it. This opened her eyes, and she offered the fruit to her husband, undoubtedly embellishing the offer with the same lie the devil had used on her. Adam is sometimes called the "Federal Head of the Human Race." When he committed sin, he doomed all those who followed him to exile from paradise. Indeed, God said, "The man has now eaten from the Tree of the Knowledge of Good and Evil. He must now leave the garden lest he partake of the Tree of Life" (my paraphrase). Adam was condemned to a lifetime of back-breaking labor—blood, sweat, and tears. And Eve was told that she would bring forth children in suffering. Then God cast the two fallen examples of the human race out of paradise and placed an angel at the gate to prevent their return.

In the Garden of Eden, in the presence of God, sin could not exert a powerful pull on Adam. To use a modern phrase, Adam was in "moral neutral." The medieval theologians put it this way: *posse non peccare*, which means "able not to sin." Had Adam continued to resist the urge to break his only commandment, would he have been so established in righteousness that he would have been *non posse peccare*? The seven billion human beings who now inhabit this planet could strongly wish so. But we will never know the answer until it is revealed to us on Judgment Day.

Only when Jesus Christ, the Son of God, came to Earth and lived a sinless life and died for the sins of mankind were we freed from the curse brought upon us by the first man, Adam.

God was dealing with fallen humanity. With the advent of the Savior, the Holy Spirit powerfully manifested in the lives of Christian people in an apparent struggle against the power of demonic spirits seeking to destroy them as creatures made in the image of God. With that in mind, I want to turn our attention now to the Old Testament. It chronicles the remarkable encounters of holy men and women before the time of Jesus Christ—touched by God's Holy Spirit moving throughout the earth to bring about God's plans for mankind.

OLD COVENANT

CHAPTER 4

HE WHO CAUSES
EVERYTHING TO BE

The stain of sin quickly corrupted the two fallen humans, Adam and Eve. Adam made love to his wife, Eve, and she became pregnant and gave birth to Cain. Later she gave birth to his brother Abel. According to the narrative, Abel kept flocks and Cain tilled the soil. Each brought an offering to the Lord. But God accepted Abel's offering of a sacrificial animal while rejecting Cain's offering of the produce of his field. Cain's offering, on its face, appeared to be made up of fleshly endeavor, whereas Abel's offering appeared to come from sacrificial grace. So Cain grew jealous, and when an opportunity presented itself, he attacked Abel and killed him.

The rapid progression of sin is apparent—first simple disobedience, then shame before God, then jealousy and resentment, outright anger, and ultimately murder. Who can forget Cain's answer to the Lord regarding his brother's absence: "Am I my brother's keeper?" (Genesis 4:9 NIV).

Through the years, people have read the account of how the Israelites took over pagan territory and followed God's instruction to exterminate the people in it. In a very short period of time, God witnessed the rapid spread of sin and the horrible consequences that flowed from it. To our modern minds, such genocide seems inconceivable, but a holy God intent on preserving the integrity of a holy people could not permit the emergence of a contagion among them which ultimately would have resulted in their permanent downfall. In the mind of a wise God, a deadly contagion like the coronavirus pandemic of 2020 could not be reasoned with or persuaded to change its way. It had to be eradicated.

According to Genesis 4:25, Adam made love to his wife again, and she gave birth to a son named Seth, saying, "God has granted me another child in place of Abel, since Cain killed him" (NIV). But what it says next is something I consider to be earth-shattering: Genesis 4:26 states, "At that time, people began to call on the name of the LORD [YHWH]" (NIV).

Why is that verse so significant to Genesis? Throughout the English version of the Old Testament, whenever we find the capital letters L-O-R-D, we know that is not an accurate translation of the Hebrew texts. In the actual texts, the name of the One worshiped is not "Lord," but "YHWH." These Hebrew letters, Y-H-W-H, are the holy name of God. But again, what does this name mean?

When a voice spoke to Moses from the burning bush and called him to go to the land of Egypt, he wanted to know what to tell the people if they asked what the name of the One who sent him was, the One who instructed him to do those things.

God replied, "I AM WHO I AM. This is what you are to say to the Israelites: 'I AM has sent me to you'" (Exodus 3:13 NIV).

It's my understanding that the tetragrammaton YHWH comprises the Hiphil tense of the verb phrase "to be." That, in turn, can be translated into English as "He who causes everything to be." The covenant name of God given to humanity after the birth of the third child of Adam and Eve was no longer Elohim, which we learned about at the creation, but YHWH, translated into English as "He who causes everything to be."

As we back up to creation, we see God, we see the Spirit of God, and we see the Word of God. Bringing this forward, the Father in the Trinity is the Supreme Mind, the Son is the Word of God through whom the Father expresses Himself, and the Spirit is the One who deals with the creation and actually brings things to pass. Therefore, I do not feel it is too much of a stretch intellectually to say that "He who causes everything to be" is actually the name of the Holy Spirit. To the covenant people of God, the Lord they are to acknowledge in the new covenant is the Holy Spirit Himself, under the name YHWH.

With this in mind, we can read the Old Testament in a totally new light. For example, in Deuteronomy 29 (NIV), we read, "These are the terms of the covenant [YHWH] commanded Moses to make with the Israelites in Moab" (verse 1). This is the covenant of "Him who causes everything to be." The Holy Spirit is the One who told Moses what covenant to make on behalf of the Israelites, and then Moses went on to say, "Your eyes have seen all that the LORD [He who causes everything to be] did in Egypt to Pharaoh" (verse 2). Again, the Holy Spirit caused plagues in Egypt and brought forth deliverance of the people of God. In verses 10–13, Moses said,

> All of you are standing today in the presence of the LORD [YHWH] your God—your leaders and chief men, your elders and officials, and all the other men of Israel, together with your children and your wives, and the foreigners living in your camps who chop your wood and carry your water. You are standing here in order to enter into a covenant with the LORD [YHWH] your God, a covenant the LORD [YHWH] is making with you this day and sealing with an oath, to confirm you this day as his people, that he may be your God as he promised you and as he swore to your fathers, Abraham, Isaac, and Jacob. (NIV)

Then in verse 29, Moses said, "The secret things belong to the LORD [YHWH] our God, but the things revealed belong to us and to our children forever, that we may follow all the words of this law."

Finally, in Deuteronomy 31:1–2, Moses told the people that he was 120 years old and God had forbidden him to cross the Jordan, but he encouraged the Israelites with these words in verses 3–6:

> The LORD [YHWH] your God himself will cross over ahead of you. He will destroy these nations before you, and you will take possession of their land. Joshua also will cross over ahead of you, as the

LORD [YHWH] said. And the LORD [YHWH] will do to them what he did to Sihon and Og, the kings of the Amorites, whom he destroyed along with their land. The LORD [YHWH] will deliver them to you, and you must do to them all that I have commanded you. Be strong and courageous. Do not be afraid or terrified because of them, for the LORD [YHWH] your God goes with you; he will never leave you nor forsake you. (NIV)

Can we understand how revolutionary this concept is? If indeed the Holy Spirit is "He who causes everything to be," then the Holy Spirit would choose a new leader for Israel and be with him, stilling all his enemies before him if he was strong and courageous. I marvel at the strength this gives us as God's people when we realize that the Spirit of God will go like a mighty warrior before us, so that none of our enemies can stand against us. If we obey Him, all things are possible. The power of the Holy Spirit is beyond human comprehension, and His Hebrew name describes it: He who causes everything to be.

I believe the book of Joshua shows even more poignantly the interplay between the Holy Spirit and the nation of Israel, keeping in mind that the English word LORD is not a faithful translation of the Hebrew tetragrammaton YHWH. The Book of Joshua is a ringing affirmation of how the Spirit of God will remain beside His people if they are strong and courageous.

Think of these words from the beginning of Joshua 1, where YHWH said to Moses's aid Joshua, the son of Nun,

Moses my servant is dead. Now then, you and all these people, get ready to cross the Jordan River into the land I am about to give them.... As I was with Moses, so I will be with you; I will never leave you nor forsake you. Be strong and courageous, because you will lead these people to inherit the land I swore to their ancestors to give them....

Have I not commanded you? Be strong and courageous. Do not be afraid; do not be discouraged, for the LORD [YHWH] your God will be with you wherever you go. (Joshua 1:2, 5–6, 9 NIV)

This book is about the Holy Spirit, but we see in the Old Testament how the dramatic presence of the Holy Spirit directs, sustains, encourages, and defends God's people. And all of this took place before the coming of the Son of God, His death on the cross, His ascension into Heaven, and His promise that He would send the Holy Spirit in power to be with His people. If the Holy Spirit was present in mighty power to speak to Moses and Joshua and lead the armies of Israel into the Promised Land, think how much more the Holy Spirit will bless those who have given their hearts to Jesus and are filled with His power at this moment.

An even more dramatic example of the relationship of the Holy Spirit with His people is found in a miracle performed by Joshua after a mighty victory over five Amorite kings. As their armies fled, we read in Joshua 10:11 that YHWH hurled large hailstones down on them. As evening fell,

Joshua said to the LORD [YHWH] in the presence of Israel, "Sun, stand still over Gibeon, and you, moon, over the valley of Aijalon." So the sun stood still, and the moon stopped, until the nation avenged itself on its enemies.... There has never been a day like it before or since, a day when the LORD [YHWH] listened to a human being. Surely the LORD [YHWH] was fighting for Israel! (Joshua 10:12–14 NIV)

Imagine the power that God manifested in order to fulfill the prayer of His servant. The rotation of this giant planet actually slowed down for a long period of time at the voice of one of God's people, activated by He who causes everything to be.

I can think of no greater demonstration of the magnificent power entrusted to God's people by the Holy Spirit. As I write this book, I feel that I am personally on the edge of something enormously wonderful that should be available to those of us filled with the Spirit of the Living God.

CHAPTER 5

NOAH'S ARK

A s much as we wish it weren't true, the history of mankind is filled with examples of rebellion against God.

Only a few generations after Adam, there was born a man named Noah, whose name is believed to mean "comfort." Genesis tells us that Noah's parents intended him to "comfort [them] in the labor and painful toil of [their] hands caused by the ground the LORD [YHWH] has cursed" (Genesis 5:29 NIV). Yet in Noah's time there was no turning to God. In fact, we read in Genesis 6:5 that "every inclination of the thoughts of the human heart was only evil all the time" (NIV). Isn't it amazing how sin spreads like a plague and seemingly carries everything before it?

The Psalmist wrote, "Let the words of my mouth, and the meditation of my heart, be acceptable in thy sight, O LORD [YHWH], my strength, and my redeemer" (Psalm 19:14 KJV). But in the days of Noah, the opposite was true. Every thought that human beings had in those days was continuously on evil.

Scripture says that YHWH regretted that He had made human beings on the earth. I am sure some people would have said as they do now in international negotiations, "Why not reason with them and hope they will reform?" YHWH knew better. These people were too far gone. Reform was not an option. YHWH in His wisdom knew that the earth must be cleansed of its evil inhabitants, and "He who causes everything to be" would begin a new creation using the only family He found righteous in all of humanity—that of Noah and his sons.

In this instance, as is true throughout the Bible, the Holy Spirit looked for a human partner to accomplish His desires on the earth. He could have created a boat by Himself. He could have brought in the animals by Himself. He could have provided food for the animals by Himself. And He could have started a new race of humanity by Himself. Instead, He instructed Noah precisely in the type of boat to build, the materials to use, the dimensions, and what he was to put on board.

Two verses in this portion of Genesis are interesting. Verse 6:22 says, "Noah did everything just as God [Elohim] commanded him" (NIV). In the very next sentence, we read, "The LORD [YHWH] then said to Noah, 'Go into the ark, you and your whole family, because I have found you righteous in this generation'" (Genesis 7:1 NIV). Later, in verse 5, we find that Noah did all that YHWH commanded him. I frankly have no answer as to why one verse describes God as Elohim and the other refers to the Covenant Deity of YHWH. Nevertheless, it is "He who causes everything to be" who directed the building of the ark, selected the passengers for the ark, described its function, and then sealed it.

At the end of the flood, God sent a wind that dried out the earth and said to Noah, "Come out of the earth...you and your wife and your sons" (Genesis 8:16 NIV). Yet in Genesis 8:21, we read that Noah built an altar to YHWH and sacrificed burnt offerings. YHWH smelled the pleasing aroma and said in His heart, "Never again will I curse the ground because of humans, even though every inclination of the heart is evil from childhood" (NIV). It seems that in this encounter we behold the operation of the Trinity of God, both the Father and Holy Spirit, working together to cleanse the human race and then start it all over again in God's image.

CHAPTER 6

ABRAHAM, THE BLESSING TO ALL MANKIND

Through the centuries, as the human race multiplied in number and diversity, it became clear that YHWH decided to narrow His revelation to one man and his descendants. They would, in turn, be given a two-thousand-year prophetic insight, a body of what we know as Scripture. The Apostle Paul wrote to his disciple Timothy and said, "All scripture is God-breathed" (2 Timothy 3:16 NIV).

And in 2 Peter 1:21 we read, "For prophecy never had its origin in the human will, but prophets, though human, spoke from God as they were carried along by the Holy Spirit" (NIV). We see that the Holy Spirit decided to prepare for all mankind the written record of His plans, including setting the human race free from the shackles of sin by the sacrifice and resurrection of the Word of God. The Son of God, in turn, will pour out the power of the Spirit of God upon all flesh before the Triune God creates Heaven and Earth again, making all things new.

As I write this book, the religion known as Christianity, which takes its name from the Greek term for the Jewish Messiah (or *Christos*), is the largest expression of religion in the world. I was told by a consortium of Bible translators that within some thirty-six years the Bible, given to the Jewish descendants of Abraham by the Holy Spirit, will have at least a partial translation into every language on the face of the earth. Some who are looking for a clue as to when the Lord will return will find these words of Jesus Christ instructive: "This gospel of the kingdom will be preached in all the world for a witness to all the nations, and then the end will come" (Matthew 24:14 NKJV). Is it possible that in our day, the revelation of God through the Holy Spirit to mankind will include witnessing the *Parousia* (the appearance of the Son of God to deliver the kingdoms of this world to the Father, once again uniting all creation under the glorious leadership of the Triune God)?

Hundreds of years after mankind scattered, YHWH chose to set apart for Himself the family of Terah, who was the father of Abram, Haran, and Nahor. They moved from Ur of the Chaldees, deep in Mesopotamia, to the land of Canaan, probably modern-day Palestine. Then in Genesis 12:1, YHWH said to Abram, "Go from your country, your people and your father's household to the land I will show you" (NIV). In Genesis 12:2–3, we read: "I will make you into a great nation, and I will bless you; I will make your name great, and you will be a blessing. I will bless those who bless you, and whoever curses you I will curse, and all peoples on earth will be blessed through you" (NIV).

As Abram traveled south, he encountered a man named Melchizedek, a priest of God Most High. *Melchizedek* in

Hebrew means "King of Righteousness." Melchizedek blessed Abram in the name of God Most High, Creator of Heaven and Earth. Abram, in turn, gave Melchizedek a tenth of the plunder he gained in battle against the king of Sodom.

As an aside, this is often used as the template for Christian organizations who say that it's certainly biblical to tithe to a place where you are blessed.

We learn in Genesis 17 that when Abram was ninety-nine years old, YHWH appeared to him and said, "I am God Almighty. Walk before me faithfully and be blameless, and then I will make my covenant between me and you and will greatly increase your numbers" (NIV). It is clear from the Genesis account that Abram, later called Abraham (the "father of nations"), was unusually favored by YHWH. In fact, there is a remarkable occurrence in Genesis 15 when Abraham took a heifer, a goat, and a ram, along with a dove and a young pigeon, and divided them in halves, laying them on the ground. "As the sun was setting, Abraham fell into a deep sleep" (verse 12). After dark, "a smoking fire pot with a blazing torch appeared and passed between the pieces of the animals. On that day the LORD [YHWH] made a covenant with Abram and said, 'To your descendants I give this land'" (Genesis 15:17–18 NIV).

"He who causes everything to be" picked one man, Abraham, to be the father of the chosen people through his son, Isaac; Isaac's son, Jacob; and Jacob's twelve sons. God would entrust this family with His oracles, almost two millennia of history, and ultimately the arrival of the Son of God as the Savior of the world.

A particularly revealing occurrence took place when God promised Abraham that his descendants would be as numerous as the stars. The Apostle Paul in the book of Romans describes the circumstance with great poignancy. Abraham "considered not his own body" (which was nearly one hundred years old), nor "the deadness" of his wife's womb, but was "strong in faith, giving glory to God; And being fully persuaded that, what [God] had promised, he was able also to perform" (Romans 4:19–21 KJV). "Abraham 'believed God, and it was counted to Him for righteousness'" (Galatians 3:6 WEB).

YHWH had promised Abraham that he would have a son, and despite the childlessness of his wife and his own infirmity, he brought forth his son, Isaac. His name means "laughter," because Sarah laughed when she heard that she would become pregnant and give birth.

When the son of promise, Isaac, was about twelve years old, God instructed Abraham to sacrifice him at a place called Mount Moriah. Without question, God used Isaac to serve as a type of His own Son, Jesus. For Jesus was the Sacrificial Lamb, totally yielded to the will of the Father, who actually carried His own cross to Calvary, even as Isaac had carried the wood for his own sacrifice up Mount Moriah. This was probably the cruelest test that could ever be given to a human being—to plunge a knife into the heart of the object of his hopes and dreams. Yet that's what God called Abraham to do.

At the last second before the knife was to be plunged into Isaac's heart, a being known as the Angel of YHWH called out from Heaven and said to Abraham, "Don't lay a hand on the boy" (Genesis 22:12 NIV). Lo and behold, on the other side of the mountain was a ram caught in the thicket. It was to be the sacrificial offering in Isaac's stead. From that moment on, the full blessing of the Lord came upon Abraham. In Genesis 22:15–18, we read:

> The angel of the LORD [YHWH] called to Abraham from Heaven a second time and said, "I swear by myself, declares the LORD [YHWH], that because you have done this and have not withheld your son, your only son, I will surely bless you and make your descendants as numerous as the stars in the sky and as the sand on the seashore. Your descendants will take possession of the cities of their enemies, and through your offspring all nations on earth will be blessed, because you have obeyed me." (NIV)

Henceforth, although the Holy Spirit spoke from time to time to people in various circumstances, the principal revelation of the Holy Spirit was directed toward the Jewish descendants of Abraham. The Holy Scriptures, both Old and New Testaments with one exception (the Gospel of Luke), were all in the hands of the direct descendants of Abraham. As I have shown, it was the Holy Spirit, known by His covenant name of YHWH, who directed the revelation to Abraham, and who began to speak to Abraham's descendants: the prophets, kings, teachers, and temple officers. Let's now examine what they had to say about the Holy Spirit.

CHAPTER 7

A Nation Set High above the Nations

E ven as YHWH picked Abraham and his descendants as the conduit for His revelation for all humanity, we learn that YHWH carefully led the Israelites into the Promised Land. He promised them extraordinary blessings, and at the same time did not hesitate to show His wrath if they willfully ignored His express commands.

The Book of Deuteronomy is derived from two Greek words: *deuteros*, which means "second," and *nomos*, which means law. So Deuteronomy is the second recitation of God's law to people. Look how closely YHWH dealt with the Israelites:

The LORD [YHWH] your God commands you this day to follow these decrees and laws. You have declared this day that the LORD [YHWH] is your God and you will walk in obedience to Him. And the LORD [YHWH] has declared this day that you are his people,

his treasured possession as he promised. He has declared
that he will set you in praise, fame, and honor high
above all the nations he has made, and that you will be
a people holy to the LORD [YHWH] your God as he
promised. (Deuteronomy 26:16–19 NIV)

Think on these wonderful promises that flowed from
YHWH to the people of Israel, if indeed YHWH is the covenant
name of the Holy Spirit. I believe that each of my readers will
understand my personal desire that they receive the blessings the
Holy Spirit will bestow on His chosen people.

Consider these words found near the beginning of Deuteronomy 28:

The LORD [YHWH] your God will set you high
above all the nations on earth....

You will be blessed in the city and blessed in the
country.

The fruit of your womb will be blessed, and the
crops of your land and the young of your livestock—the
calves of your herds and the lambs of your flock.

Your basket and your kneading trough will be
blessed.

You will be blessed when you come in and blessed
when you go out.

The LORD [YHWH] will grant that the enemies
who rise up against you will be defeated before you.
They will come at you from one direction but flee from
you in seven.

The LORD [YHWH] will send a blessing on your barns and on everything you put your hand to. The LORD [YHWH] your God will bless you in the land he is giving you.

The LORD [YHWH] will establish you as his holy people, as he promised you on oath, if you keep the commands of the LORD [YHWH] your God and walk in obedience to him. Then all the peoples on earth will see that you are called by the name of the LORD [YHWH], and they will fear you. The LORD [YHWH] will grant you abundant prosperity—in the fruit of your womb, the young of your livestock and the crops of your ground—in the land he swore to your ancestors to give you.

The LORD [YHWH] will open the heavens, the storehouse of his bounty, to send rain on your land in season and to bless all the work of your hands. You will lend to many nations but will borrow from none. The LORD [YHWH] will make you the head, not the tail. If you pay attention to the command of the LORD [YHWH] your God that I give you this day and carefully follow them, you will always be at the top, never at the bottom. Do not turn aside from any of the commands I give you today, to the right or to the left, following other gods and serving them. (Deuteronomy 28:1, 3–14 NIV)

Can our imagination comprehend the blessings that the Holy Spirit will give us if we obey Him and follow His leading?

He will lift us up, He will prosper us, He will keep us in health, and He will answer our prayers. Since all the world belongs to the Holy Spirit, He obviously does not need a committee meeting to determine the recipient of His blessings. I believe each of us should repeat over and over again the promises that He made to Moses.

Although, of course, the physical descendants of Abraham are the heirs of the promises made by the Holy Spirit to Abraham, I think it is fair to say that those of us who are linked to the Messiah of Israel are also the spiritual children of Abraham. And I, for one, am claiming His promises. Keep in mind the Holy Spirit is never diminished. He is infinite. If He pours out blessings on you, He can also pour out blessings on me. If He pours out blessings on your neighbor or on his business or family, He has sufficient resources at His disposal as an infinite God to reward each one of us with the blessings enumerated in Deuteronomy 28.

In conclusion of the marvelous message that YHWH gave Moses to deliver to the people, He gave this final charge in Deuteronomy 30:15–20:

> See, I set before you today life and prosperity, death and destruction. For I command you today to love the LORD [YHWH] your God, to walk in obedience to him, and to keep his commands, decrees, and laws; then you will live and increase, and the LORD [YHWH] your God will bless you in the land you are entering to possess....
>
> Now choose life, so that you and your children may live and that you may love the LORD [YHWH] your

God, listen to his voice, and hold fast to him. For the LORD [YHWH] is your life and he will give you many years in the land he swore to give to your fathers, Abraham, Isaac and Jacob. (NIV)

It is clear to me that the words of the Holy Spirit given to and through Moses come to us today with the same power they held on the day they were first uttered. And with our Jewish friends, I say, "*L'chaim*" ("to life"). Let us all choose life under the benevolent care of the exalted Holy Spirit, who will never leave us or forsake us.

The people of God over the years have been confronted by satanic power and the evils of fellow human beings who have not hesitated to arrest, torture, imprison, and kill them. The Apostle Paul told us that there will be many pressures upon us as we enter the Kingdom of God. To be sure, God intends blessings for the children of Abraham and those who share in their inheritance. But we also must understand that there's a titanic struggle taking place in the heavenlies between an all-powerful Creator and the one called the "prince of the power of the air." The Jesus we serve—the matchless Son of God—was permitted to suffer a horrible death on the cross and bear the penalty for the sin of mankind. Now we enter into His blessings, and I urge everyone who reads this book to realize that we are indeed seated in heavenly places in Christ Jesus. We must claim for ourselves God's promises and His blessings, knowing full well that some may indeed share in the fate of the Apostle Paul, who suffered unbelievable trials while bringing us his message, or the Apostle Peter, who in his later years was crucified in Rome.

CHAPTER 8

KING DAVID FORETELLS THE MESSIAH

We have shown that the Holy Spirit chose a man named Abraham to bring forth the family to record His message to the world and ultimately be the human vehicle for the emergence of the Word of God, the Messiah who would die for the redemption of mankind.

Certainly, the descendants of Abraham gained special favor with YHWH. One of those was a king named David, who was said to be "a man after [God's] own heart" (1 Samuel 13:14 NIV). The relationship David had with the Holy Spirit was profound. We find in 1 Chronicles 14:2 that "David knew that the LORD [YHWH] had established him as king over Israel, and that his kingdom had been highly exalted for the sake of His people Israel" (NIV). In verse 17 of the same chapter, we read, "David's fame spread throughout every land, and the LORD [YHWH] made all the nations fear him." We see here clearly that the blessing of the Holy Spirit can exalt one that He favors. And when that person happens to be the head of a country, the Holy Spirit will actually bring fear of him to all the surrounding nations. The Holy Spirit gave David wonderful psalms of praise. It seems that the Lord had lifted David's spirit to a level of exultation, which is rare for any human being.

After David won a capital in Zion, he began to make plans to construct a temple—not to contain the God of Creation, but to honor the name of YHWH. Yet the Bible tells us that Nathan the prophet received the word of God, which said, "Go and tell my servant David, this is what the LORD [YHWH] says, 'You are not the one to build me a house to dwell in'" (1 Chronicles 17:4 NIV). And from 2 Samuel 7:

> I took you from the pasture, from tending the flock, and appointed you ruler over my people Israel.... Now I will make your name great, like the names of the greatest men on earth. And I will provide a place for my people Israel and will plant them so that they can have a home of their own....
>
> The LORD [YHWH] himself will establish a house for you...I will raise up your offspring to succeed you.... He is the one who will build a house for my Name, and I will establish the throne of his kingdom forever. (2 Samuel 7:8–13 NIV)

1 Chronicles 17 tells us this:

> Then King David went in and sat before the LORD [YHWH] and he said, "Who am I LORD [YHWH]

God, and what is my family, that you have brought me thus far?... You, LORD [YHWH] God, have looked on me as though I were the most exalted of men.... For the sake of your servant and according to your will, you have done this great thing and made known all these great promises.

"There is no one like you, LORD [YHWH], and there is no God but you, as we have heard with our own ears." (1 Chronicles 17:16–17, 19–20 NIV)

This shows the most incredible intimacy between the Holy Spirit and His servant David. It provides a model for people of all ages to realize that the Holy Spirit is not a deity far off but is completely approachable by those who love Him. We also see here that the Holy Spirit grants to His servants not only promises of immediate blessing, but also knowledge of far-off events.

Out of the relationship between David and YHWH, there came forth several psalms which give precise details about the crucifixion of Jesus. These so-called *Messianic Psalms* are clearly prophetic and clearly energized by the Spirit of God. I believe David wrote them without even realizing that he was actually describing the sufferings of Jesus Christ, the anointed Messiah and Son of God.

Consider these words from the twenty-second Psalm, which describes almost word for word what happened to Jesus Christ on the cross:

All who seek me mock me; they hurl insults, shaking their heads. "He trusts in the LORD [YHWH]," they say, "let the LORD [YHWH] deliver him, since he delights in him."...

Do not be far from me, for trouble is near and there is no one to help.... I am poured out like water, and all my bones are out of joint. My heart has turned to wax; it has melted within me. My mouth is dried up like a potsherd, and my tongue sticks to the roof of my mouth.... All my bones are on display; people stare and gloat over me. They divide my clothes among them and cast lots for my garment. (Psalm 22:7–8, 11, 14–15, 17–18 NIV)

There is also the fifty-first Psalm, where David confesses to the Lord the sins of adultery with Bathsheba and the murder of her husband, Uriah. David confesses his sins before the Lord and asks to be cleansed. He says to God, "Restore to me the joy of your salvation and grant me a willing spirit" (verse 12 NIV). He also says, "Take not thy holy spirit from me" (verse 11 KJV). Because of his sins, David had lost his joy, and he came with a humble and broken spirit, asking God to cleanse him and restore a right relationship with Him. I doubt very seriously if the presence of the Holy Spirit would have been taken from David because of his egregious sins. But he had lost his joy and his walk with the Lord. From what I gather in reading Psalm 51, the Holy Spirit was still with him and would continue to be with him.

And consider Psalm 110, where David writes, "The LORD [YHWH] says to my Lord: 'Sit at my right hand until I make your enemies a footstool for your feet'" (verse 1 NIV). Clearly, the Holy Spirit was giving inspiration to David. The Spirit of God led David to speak the words of YHWH to the ruler he had placed in charge of Israel.

The prophetic messages given to certain holy men were not just limited to David. I should also mention the prophet Isaiah, who I believe was led by the Holy Spirit. Isaiah 53 is written as if the Holy Spirit enabled him, as a man of God, to enter the sufferings of Jesus Christ on the cross. The prophet writes in verse 5, "He was pierced for our transgressions, he was crushed for our iniquities; the punishment that brought us peace was on him, and by his wounds we are healed" (NIV). Here you have the piercing of Jesus's hands, feet, and side. You have His back shredded by a vicious cat-o'-nine-tails wielded by a brutal Roman soldier.

In 53:8–9, "He was cut off from the land of the living; for the transgression of my people he was punished. He was assigned a grave with the wicked and with the rich in his death" (NIV). In truth, Jesus Christ was laid in the tomb of a wealthy man near the Garden of Gethsemane. Long before these things happened, the Holy Spirit moved Isaiah to write about them. I feel sure that Isaiah did not comprehend the subject for whom these words were intended. It had to come from direct revelation.

But there is something even more astounding. Consider these words: "Yet it was the LORD's [YHWH's] will to crush him and cause him to suffer, and though the LORD [YHWH] makes his life an offering for sin.... After he has suffered he will see the light of life and be satisfied" (Isaiah 53:10–11 NIV). Earlier we read, "We all, like sheep, have gone astray; each of us has turned to our own way; and the LORD [YHWH] has laid on him the iniquities of us all" (Isaiah 53:6 NIV).

Now consider the full impact of these verses. We have learned in other parts of Scripture that God Himself said of Jesus

Christ, "This is my beloved Son, in whom I am well pleased" (Matthew 3:17 NKJV). We also learned from the first chapter of the Gospel of John that "In the beginning was the Word [or the Son of God], and the Word was with God, and the Word was God" (verse 1 NIV). If my analysis is correct, the LORD [YHWH] of the Old Testament is actually the Holy Spirit.

So what Isaiah is saying in this extraordinary chapter is that it was the will of the Father to crush the Son of God, causing Him to suffer to "justify man" and to "bear their iniquities." Then YHWH will bring Him to life again. You remember the words of Jesus on the cross when He called out in Aramaic, "*Eloi! Eloi! Lema sabachthani?*" which means, "My God, My God! Why have You forsaken Me?" (Mark 15:34 NIV). What Isaiah portrays in the fifty-third chapter is a cosmic event. It isn't merely the description of a man on earth. It is the cleansing of the sin of an entire universe by the death of the Son of God, willed by the Father, and brought about by the agency of the Holy Spirit. We may infer that in the depth of the wisdom of the Godhead, it was necessary for one member to willingly sacrifice Himself to bring about the cleansing and redemption of the entire universe. Indeed, Jesus died on the cross for you. Jesus died on the cross for me. Jesus died on the cross for all mankind.

Jesus, as the Son of God, died on the cross to bring redemption not only to the human race, but to all of creation.

Before His ascension into Heaven, Jesus told His disciples, "All authority in heaven and on earth has been given to me" (Matthew 28:18 NIV). His authority extends to you and me, and it also extends to all the planets and galaxies throughout this vast universe in which we make our home.

CHAPTER 9

MEN FILLED WITH WISDOM
AND UNDERSTANDING

The Holy Spirit of God, as we have seen, is the member of the Trinity who was given the task of creating this incredible universe in which we live. His skill is beyond measure, and His ability to bring forth remarkable things in our universe is beyond reason. Therefore, it should not be surprising that throughout the history of mankind, the Holy Spirit has given to select individuals the power to craft tools, implements, fabrics, and countless items of utility and beauty.

I draw our attention to the Book of Exodus in the Old Testament, where we read,

> Moses said to the Israelites, "See, the LORD [YHWH] has chosen Bezalel son of Uri, the son of Hur, of the tribe of Judah, and He has filled him with the Spirit of God with wisdom, and understanding, and with all kinds of skills—to make artistic designs for work in gold, silver

and bronze, to cut and set stones, to work in wood and engage in all kinds of artistic crafts. And he has given both him and Oholiab, son of Ahisamach, of the tribe of Dan, to teach others. He has filled them with skill to do all kinds of work as engravers, designers, embroiderers in blue, purple and scarlet yarn and fine linen, and weavers—all of them skilled workers and designers. So Bezalel, Oholiab and every skilled person to whom the LORD [YHWH] has given skill and ability to know how to carry out all of the work of constructing the sanctuary are to do the work just as the LORD [YHWH] has commanded." (Exodus 35:30–35, 36:1 NIV)

Read any secular text you choose, and you will find a gap in the credibility of primitive Neanderthals' evolving into a complex society using increasingly complex tools and implements. The truth is that these skills did not "evolve." They were given to mankind by the Holy Spirit of God. It is His Spirit who has led, consciously or unconsciously, the human race into increasing sophistication and complexity.

Some years ago, I began an amateur study of hand-woven carpets. My appreciation of each nation grew in measure as I learned of the marvelous vegetable dyes used in carpet thread, the elegant designs that appeared in the carpets, and the remarkable skill that brought forth beautiful carpets, some with more than five hundred hand-sewn knots per square inch.

I have been to India, where some people in the primitive areas live in huts with dirt floors, and yet the women wear simply glorious saris with brilliant colors.

Think of the distinguished men of science—such as Isaac Newton, Louis Pasteur, and Albert Einstein—and thousands of others like them whose minds were able to grasp a little piece of God's universe to improve the civilizations in which they lived.

In our modern era, I am reminded of a son of slaves, George Washington Carver, who was brought up in a Christian home to love and serve Jesus Christ. Carver, in his humble way, prayed this simple prayer to the God he served: "Mr. Creator, show me the secrets of Your universe." God replied, "Little man, you can't handle the secrets of My universe, but I will show you the secrets of the peanut." To this, Carver asked, "Mr. Creator, what should I do with the peanut?" And God replied, "Take it apart and then put it back together again." Out of this simple prayer came an incredible array of paints, plastics, and foods which completely revolutionized the agriculture of the South, along with the Carver-manipulated soybean. Again, I reiterate that these discoveries did not evolve. They flowed from the creativity of the Holy Spirit given to one of His willing servants.

Think also of the brilliant composers such as Bach, Handel, Beethoven, and Brahms, whose minds were transformed to enable them to hear each instrument of an orchestra and bring forth the necessary notes for glorious symphonies and oratorios.

It is the Holy Spirit, working through the centuries, who brings to those creatures made in God's image revelations that have exceeded what they could have learned from their physical surroundings.

Yet beyond that, we all have a yearning for an afterlife with God throughout eternity. As the Apostle Paul wrote, "'Eye has not seen, nor ear heard, nor have entered into the heart of man the things which God has prepared for those who love Him.' But God has revealed them to us by His Spirit. For the Spirit searches all things, yes, the deep things of God" (1 Corinthians 2:9–10 NKJV).

I want to emphasize again that God is not limited. And since He is infinite, His creativity is available to every single one of those who are His children.

The Apostle Paul wrote to the Corinthians to "earnestly desire the best gifts" (1 Corinthians 12:31 NKJV). God wants us to be happy and live an abundant life. The Holy Spirit can fulfill our deepest longings if we are only willing to believe in Him, to trust Him, and to obey His commandments.

CHAPTER 10

TWO REMARKABLE PROPHETS

I now want to turn our attention to two remarkable men in Israel who have been called prophets. The Holy Spirit moved upon them in a fashion that more clearly resembles some of the activity of the Spirit of God in His Church in our modern era. These men are Elijah and Elisha.

The first, Elijah, has an interesting name which is universally mispronounced by those of us in the West. We call him ee-LI-ja. This, however, is not his name in Hebrew. His name is EL-i-yah. *El* is the Hebrew name for "God," *I* is possessive, and *yah* means "YHWH." So the prophet's real name is "My God is YHWH." The other prophet, Elisha (EL-i-sha), means "My God is salvation." These two men, under the power of God, brought forth amazing miracles.

Elijah contended with the priests of Baal, calling down fire from Heaven on a sacrifice on Mount Carmel. When there was a drought in Israel, Elijah got on his knees and prayed over and over again, until a small cloud appeared in the skies that soon turned into a violent rainstorm, breaking the drought that had crippled the country. Elijah chose Elisha as his pupil and associate. As they traveled together, they both shared the miracles of God's Spirit.

The time came when YHWH determined to take Elijah from the earth. A company of prophets realized what was going to happen, and Elisha confirmed their sense of it. As we read the narrative, it's somewhat amusing that Elisha absolutely refused to let Elijah out of his sight, even though Elijah tried repeatedly to be left alone.

Finally, as his departure grew near, Elijah asked Elisha what favor he would like to receive. Elisha said, "Let me inherit a double portion of your spirit." This was asking a lot, because Elijah had performed extraordinary miracles and had been visited by the Spirit of God repeatedly. So he said to Elisha, "You have asked a difficult thing...yet if you see me when I am taken from you, it will be yours" (2 Kings 2:9–10 NIV).

What an example for us today to seek after God's power despite all obstacles and circumstances—to be undeterred by those who tell us it can't be done, who tell us our spiritual desire is a hard thing. How many times have I personally been told that the course God laid out for me was an impossibility? Elisha refused to take no for an answer—just as we learned in the story of Jacob, who wrestled with an angel and refused to let him go until he received a blessing.

These words of Jesus come to us in the present tense of the Greek language: keep on asking, keep on seeking, keep on knocking. "Ask and it will be given to you; seek and you will find;

knock and the door will be opened to you" (Matthew 7:7 NIV). This is called importunate prayer, and Elisha had mastered it.

As Elijah and Elisha approached a river, Elijah took his cloak and struck the water. The water parted, and the two men walked across on dry land. A little farther along, a fiery chariot appeared from Heaven, and Elijah was caught up to Heaven in a whirlwind. In the process, his cloak fell to the ground. Elisha picked it up, rolled it up, approached the stream they had forded before, and called out, "Where is the God of Elijah?" (2 Kings 2:14 NKJV). As he struck the surface, the waters parted and he went across on dry land.

We learn in the Bible that the Holy Spirit enabled Elisha to perform twice as many miracles as Elijah. He asked for twice as much, and he got what he asked for. Now let's take a look at how the Holy Spirit enabled Elisha to perform miraculous deeds after he received a double portion of the Spirit on Elijah—which we must assume was the Holy Spirit of God.

1. **Healing of the water.** In a city near Jericho, the people said to Elisha, "The water is bad and the land is unproductive" (2 Kings 2:19 NIV). Elisha took salt and made a prophetic utterance. "The LORD [YHWH] says, 'I have healed this water'" (2 Kings 2:21 NIV). The water has remained pure to this day.

2. **YHWH defends His prophet.** As Elisha was walking near Bethel, a group of young boys began to jeer him. His next action would hardly have been considered Christlike. He called a curse on them in the name of YHWH, and two bears appeared and devoured the youth according to the word spoken by the prophet.

3. **Military victory.** Three kings, including the king of Israel, had marched against Moab. The armies ran out of water after

seven days and were facing death. Elisha asked for a harpist, and "the hand of the LORD [YHWH] came upon him.... 'For thus says the LORD [YHWH]: "...that valley shall be filled with water.... And this is a simple matter in the sight of the LORD [YHWH]"'" (2 Kings 3:15, 17–18 NKJV). As he spoke it, the dry land filled with water. The Moabites viewed the water as blood and rushed into an Israeli ambush in which they were slaughtered.

4. The widow's oil. The widow of one of Elisha's prophets was threatened by her creditors. Elisha told her to gather all the pots she could get her hands on, then take the little oil she had and begin pouring. As she poured, the oil multiplied until every pot was full, the oil could be sold, and the creditors satisfied.

5. The widow's son restored to life. A well-to-do lady set up a "prophet's chamber" so Elisha would have a place to rest on his journeys. Elisha asked his assistant, Gehazi, what he could do to help the lady, and Gehazi said, "She has no son, and her husband is old" (2 Kings 4:14 NIV). As the woman stood before him, Elisha prophesied under the anointing of the Holy Spirit and said, "About this time next year, you will hold a son in your arms" (2 Kings 4:16 NIV). In a year's time, she not only became pregnant, but gave birth to a son, even as Elisha had prophesied.

However, as the boy grew a bit older, he suffered what was probably a stroke and died. When word of this tragedy reached Elisha, he sent his servant to the grieving woman and then soon came himself. When Elisha arrived at the house, he found the dead boy laid on a couch. He went in, shut the door on the two of them, and prayed to YHWH. He stretched himself upon the boy once, then walked back and forth in the room, and repeated the maneuver. The dead boy sneezed seven times and sat up. The prophet's prayer was answered, and as an instrument of YHWH he brought the dead back to life.

6. Death in the pot. Elisha's disciples had gathered some gourds and other vegetables to make a stew so that they could have lunch. Apparently, one of the gourds was poisonous and the prophets could not eat it. Elisha then boldly said, "Bring me some flour" (2 Kings 4:41 NLT). He threw the flour into the pot and the poison vanished, making the stew healthy to eat.

7. Feeding a hundred. In another instance, a man came to Elisha with a basket of twenty barley loaves. I imagine they were about the size of the pita bread pockets served in Middle Eastern restaurants. "'How can I set this before a hundred men?' his servant asked. But Elisha answered, 'Give it to the people to eat. For this is what the LORD [YHWH] says, "They will eat and have some left over"'" (2 Kings 4:43 NIV). Indeed, every man had his fill and there were remnants left over. This was again much like what we saw in the days of Jesus, when He took a little boy's lunch of five loaves and two fish and fed five thousand people.

8. Naaman healed. The king of Aram (which corresponds to modern-day Syria) had in his army a general named Naaman. Naaman became afflicted with leprosy, with all of the social problems that leprosy entails. In 2 Kings 5, a little servant girl they had captured from Israel told Naaman's wife, "If only my master would see the prophet who is in Samaria! He would cure him of his leprosy" (verse 3 NIV). Naaman approached the king, who then wrote the king of Israel a letter which said, "I am sending my servant Naaman to you so that you may cure him of his leprosy" (verse 6 NIV). Of course, the king of Israel was horrified. He couldn't heal anybody of anything, so he presumed this message was merely a trick to start a war. Naaman, in all of his military finery and with a contingent of troops, arrived at the door of Elisha's dwelling, and in what would have seemed like the ultimate snub, the prophet sent a servant to the general and said simply, "Go, wash yourself seven times in the Jordan, and your flesh will be restored and you will be cleansed" (verse 10 NIV). At this, Naaman was furious. "I thought that he would surely come out to me and stand and call on the name of the LORD [YHWH] his God, wave his hand over the spot and cure me of my leprosy. Are not Abana ad Pharpar, the rivers of Damascus, better than all the waters of Israel?" (verses 11–12 NIV). He charged off in a mighty huff.

Isn't this like so many of us today? We have a preconceived notion of what God should do to save us, to bless us, to prosper us, to instruct us. If the Holy Spirit doesn't do it our way, we don't want it done at all.

Throughout history, generals, heads of state, and high officials have begun to think more highly of themselves than they ought. I remember when I was involved in seeking public office that I was attacked for believing in a higher power than the president of the United States. One of my articulate supporters said very cogently, "Wouldn't we be better off with a president who believes in a higher power than one who thinks he is the Higher Power?"

Despite Naaman's rage and hurt pride, one of his younger officers said, "My father, if a prophet had told you to do some great thing, would you not have done it? How much more, then, when he tells you, 'Wash and be cleansed!'" (2 Kings 5:13 NIV). In our world, we would have said, "Commander, what have you got to lose by doing this simple thing?" So Naaman humbled himself, dipped in the Jordan River, and came out of the water completely healed of his leprosy. He hurried back to the house of Elisha to thank him and offered a gift in exchange for this wonderful miracle. Elisha answered with these words, "As surely as the LORD [YHWH] lives, whom I serve, I will not accept a thing" (2 Kings 5:16 NIV). Even though Naaman urged him, he refused. "Go in peace," the prophet told him, and with that, this proud warrior became a humble servant of YHWH, the Most High God.

9. **Gehazi's duplicity.** Elisha's servant, Gehazi, heard this interchange and thought of how foolish it was to refuse a gift from this general. Without telling Elisha, he ran after Naaman and said, "My master sent me to say, 'Two young men from the company of the prophets have just come to me.... Please give them a talent of silver...with two sets of clothing'" (2 Kings 5:22 NIV). Of course, Naaman was willing to give this small gift and much more. But Gehazi took the money and the clothes and hid them in his home without telling Elisha. When Elisha questioned him, Gehazi lied. Then Elisha said, "Was not my spirit with you when the man got down from his chariot to meet you?" (2 Kings 5:26 NIV).

The Spirit of God gave Elisha what the New Testament refers to as a "word of knowledge" to learn the existence of things not available to the five senses. But Elisha was not finished. Speaking by the power of the Holy Spirit, he said to Gehazi, "Naaman's leprosy will cling to you and to your descendants forever" (2 Kings 5:27 NIV). In this case, the Holy Spirit gave His servant not only the power of knowing events not available to the senses, but the power to heal diseases and, in retribution, to speak a curse that brought on a disease. ·

10. **The axe that floats.** The company of prophets came to Elisha with requests to expand their quarters into an adjoining wooded area. They began to chop down trees to clear the land and provide the necessary timber for the dwelling. As they were chopping, the axe-head fell into the Jordan River. This implement was rare and sorely needed. So Elisha cut a stick in the shape of an axe handle and dropped it in the water. The axe-head floated up to the surface, and Elisha instructed the men to pick it up. In this example, the Holy Spirit at the command of the prophet either changed the consistency of an iron axe-head to become buoyant or the characteristics of the surrounding water were somehow changed. This is a smaller microcosm of the miracle experienced by Jesus Christ when He was seen walking on the water of the Sea of Galilee and rescued the Apostle Peter, who had successfully accomplished this remarkable feat until fear took over and he began to sink.

11. **The revelation of the Aramaean camp.** When the army of Aram settled at a place of encampment, the Holy Spirit gave a "word of knowledge" to Elisha, who warned the king of Israel to avoid that fortified spot. Of course, the king of Aram presumed there was a spy in his midst. His officials said there was no spy, that this was the work of Elisha the prophet.

12. **Elisha demonstrates the discerning of spirits.** The king of Aram determined that he could successfully deploy his forces

after eliminating Elisha, so he sent a significant armed force to capture the prophet. When Elisha and his servant left their dwelling for the day, they encountered the party of armed soldiers. The servant was terrified at what was about to happen, but Elisha calmly replied, "Those with us are greater than those with them." Then he said, "Open his eyes LORD [YHWH] that he might see" (2 Kings 6:17 NIV). Then YHWH enabled the servant to see in the invisible world a multitude of horses and fiery chariots. We must conclude that an army of angelic beings surrounds us. In the New Testament, fullness of the Holy Spirit enables the "discerning of spirits," among other gifts. This is clearly not discerning merely demons; it is the ability to see into the spiritual world which surrounds us all.

13. **Aramaeans struck blind.** The Bible says, "Elisha prayed to the LORD [YHWH] and said, 'Strike this army with blindness'" (2 Kings 6:18 NIV). And in that instant, the army could not see. Elisha went up to them and said, "I will take you to the one you are looking for." He then led them into the middle of Samaria, where their eyes were opened and they understood they had been taken captive.

We see the Apostle Paul using his exact command when he withstood the sorcerer Bar-Jesus, who was attempting to steal the word of God from the Roman proconsul Sergius Paulus. Paul, the Bible tells us, was "filled with the Holy Spirit" (Acts 13:9 NIV) and said, "You are a child of the devil.... Now the hand of the Lord is against you. You are going to be blind for a time" (Acts 13:10–11 NIV). And indeed he was.

14. **Famine lifted in besieged Samaria.** During the ongoing struggle between Aram and Israel, Ben-Hadad of Aram besieged

Samaria and cut off all its food supplies. People began dying of starvation. There was such a shortage of food that a little container of seed pods from the droppings of doves sold for five shekels. Of course, as often happens, secular authorities blamed the disaster on God. (It's amazing that we still call natural disasters "acts of God.")

As a result, the king of Israel determined to capture and kill Elisha, but the Holy Spirit warned His prophet about this. The king said, "This disaster is from the LORD [YHWH]. Why should I wait for the LORD [YHWH] any longer?" (2 Kings 6:33 NIV). And Elisha declared boldly, "Hear the word of the LORD [YHWH]. This is what the LORD [YHWH] says: 'About this time tomorrow a measure of fine flour will be sold for a shekel, and two measures of barley for a shekel, at the gate of Samaria'" (2 Kings 7:1 NASB). The officer who heard this prophecy snorted in derision, saying, "Even if the LORD [YHWH] should open the floodgates of Heaven, could this happen?" (verse 2 NIV). "'You will see it with your own eyes,' answered Elisha, 'but you will not eat any of it!'" (verse 3 NIV).

YHWH cursed the Aramaeans, causing them to miraculously hear the sound of chariots and horses of a great army. They said to one another, "Look, the king of Israel has hired the Hittite and Egyptian kings to attack us" (verse 6 NIV). They got up and fled in the dusk, abandoning their tents, horses, and donkeys. They left the camp as it was and ran for their lives.

The king of Israel sent out a mounted patrol to determine the validity of the report that he heard about this. They found battle equipment, food, and supplies all the way to the Jordan River and beyond. The starving Israelites then descended on the

Aramaean encampment and feasted on what they found. Indeed, there was such plenty that the prices came down in exactly the measure the prophet had foretold. Sadly, the king's official who had scoffed at the word of YHWH's servant was trampled to death in the rush of people leaving Samaria to get to the bounty of the Aramaean camp.

15. **Elisha foretells Hazael's cruelty.** Aram was the country to the north of Israel that corresponds to the modern nation of Syria. The language of Aram was Aramaic, also spoken by Jesus Christ as a second language. The principal deity worshipped by the people of Aram was known as Hadad. The king of Aram was named Ben-Hadad, or "Son of Hadad." His prime minister was Hazael.

King Ben-Hadad grew ill and learned that the Prophet Elisha was visiting in Damascus. He sent Hazael to learn if Elisha would inquire of YHWH about his illness. When Hazael met with Elisha, Elisha demonstrated a "word of wisdom," such as those later given to the Christian Church. The Holy Spirit showed Elisha that Ben-Hadad would not recover from his disease. But beyond that, the prophet began to weep, because the Holy Spirit showed him that Hazael would succeed Ben-Hadad and would "set fire to [Israel's] fortified places, kill their young men with the sword, dash their little children to the ground, and rip open their pregnant women" (2 Kings 8:12 NIV).

"Hazael said, 'How could your servant, a mere dog, accomplish such a feat?'

"'The LORD [YHWH] has shown me that you will become king of Aram,' answered Elisha" (2 Kings 8:13 NIV).

Shortly thereafter, Hazael took a wet cloth and held it over the nose and mouth of Ben-Hadad to kill him and become the next king, just as the prophet foretold. We learn from this interchange that the Holy Spirit was at work not only in Israel, but also in the other nations, and He would give His servants the appropriate message to deliver to foreign rulers.

16. **Jehu anointed king of Israel.** As his last official act recorded in the Old Testament,

> The prophet Elisha summoned a man from the company of the prophets and said to him, "Tuck your cloak into your belt, take this flask of olive oil with you and go to Ramoth Gilead. When you get there, look for Jehu son of Jehoshaphat, the son of Nimshi. Go to him, get him away from his companions and take him into an inner room. Then take the flask and pour the oil on his head and declare, 'This is what the LORD [YHWH] says: I anoint you king over Israel.'"
>
> So the young prophet went to Ramoth Gilead....
>
> Then the prophet poured the oil on Jehu's head and declared, "This is what the LORD [YHWH], the God of Israel, says: 'I anoint you king over the LORD's [YHWH's] people Israel. You are to destroy the house of Ahab your master, and I will avenge the blood of my servants the prophets and the blood of all the LORD's [YHWH's] servants shed by Jezebel. The whole house of Ahab will perish. I will cut off from Ahab every last male in Israel—slave or free.'" (2 Kings 9:1–4, 6–8 NIV)

Then the fellow officers inquired of the message given to Jehu. He told them, "This is what the LORD [YHWH] says:

'I anoint you king over Israel.'" At that moment, they shouted in acclamation, "Jehu is King!" (verses 12–13). From then on, Jehu utterly destroyed the house of Ahab and his relatives. He then staged a massive celebration in which he killed all the priests of Baal.

Here it is clear that the Holy Spirit not only instructed prophets to bring messages to foreign leaders, but also to actively select a king for Israel, anoint him as ruler, then use him to bring divine punishment upon an evil king and his supporters, all adherents to a false religion. This certainly gives lie to the concept that God, like a heavenly Watchmaker, turned on the mechanism of the universe and then left it to run its course. The truth is that the invisible God who "causes everything to be" never took His hand off His universe. He constantly watches over it to see that His will and His plans are accomplished. As the Apostle Paul wrote in 1 Corinthians 2:16, "Who has known the mind of the Lord so as to instruct him?" (NIV).

CHAPTER 11

JONAH, NINEVEH, AND THE GREAT FISH

In the ancient world, two nations stand out—Egypt and Assyria. Much of the Old Testament narrative shows the remarkable deliverance of the people of God from bondage in Egypt, to their wandering in the desert, their entrance into the Promised Land, and ultimately their establishment of a mighty kingdom. Time and again, the Holy Spirit was present. We saw Him in the plagues of Egypt, the slaying of the firstborn not covered by blood, the guidance by a column of fire and pillar of smoke, the precise details and craftsmanship for the tabernacle in the wilderness, the Ten Commandments and the Law of God delivered to Moses on Mount Sinai, and later when Joshua led a series of brilliant battles to conquer the kings of Canaan. But what about Assyria? Was the Holy Spirit not concerned about this mighty empire? In the Book of Jonah, we see a resounding yes!

In approximately 800 BC, the kings of Assyria demonstrated cruelty that exceeded anything the mind can conceive. For example, they flayed people while they were still alive, cut the limbs off of innocent people, impaled them with stakes, and bound them together and set them on fire. Perhaps in the history of mankind to that point, there had never been such senseless barbarity.

Obviously, this conduct was a stench in the nostrils of a Holy God. Yet by 600 BC, the cruelty had abated somewhat, and YHWH decided to send a prophet to Nineveh (the capital city of Assyria) to warn the people of potential judgment.

The Book of Jonah starts with these words: "The Word of the LORD [YHWH] came to Jonah son of Amittai: 'Go to the great city of Nineveh and preach against it, because its wickedness has come up before Me'" (Jonah 1:1–2 NIV). YHWH was not just the God of Israel, nor was He just the God who dealt with the Egyptians. The conduct of the residents of the capital city of Assyria had offended YHWH, and He commissioned a prophet to tell them of His displeasure. Instead of willingly accepting this commission from the Holy Spirit, however, Jonah resisted it.

In fact, we are told that "Jonah ran away from the LORD [YHWH]" (Jonah 1:3 NIV). At this point, YHWH could have said, "I reject Jonah and will select for Myself another willing man who will carry out my plans." But YHWH was persistent. The Psalmist wrote in Psalm 139:7–10,

Whither shall I go from thy spirit? or whither shall I flee from thy presence? If I ascend up into heaven, thou art there: if I make my bed in hell, behold, thou art there. If I take the wings of the morning, and dwell in the uttermost parts of the sea; Even there shall thy hand lead me, and thy right hand shall hold me. (KJV)

The Holy Spirit fills the whole universe, and no mere mortal can escape His call or His retribution.

But Jonah tried. He thought if he got as far away from Nineveh as possible, he could escape YHWH's call on his life, so he booked passage on a ship destined for Tarshish. Tarshish was the name given to territory beyond Gibraltar, which may well have included the British Isles. This was certainly a place far distant from ancient Nineveh.

But the Bible says, "The LORD [YHWH] sent a great wind on the sea, and such a violent storm arose that the ship threatened to break up" (Jonah 1:4 NIV). The hardened sailors were terrified and began to throw cargo over the side of the ship to lighten it. Then, one by one, they began to question all the passengers. When they got to Jonah, they said, "'Who is responsible for making all this trouble for us? What kind of work do you do? Where do you come from? What is your country? From what people are you?'" (Jonah 1:8 NIV). Then Jonah, looking shame-faced, came forward and said, "I am a Hebrew and I worship the LORD [YHWH], the God of heaven who made the sea and the dry land" (Jonah 1:9 NIV). We are told that these sailors knew Jonah was running away from YHWH because YHWH had told them so. Once again, they asked Jonah what they should do, and he said, "Pick me up and throw me into the sea...and it will become calm" (Jonah 1:12 NIV).

It is amazing that these sailors had an innate sense of right and wrong, and they cried to YHWH, "LORD [YHWH], please do not let us die for taking this man's life. Do not hold us accountable for killing an innocent man, for you, LORD [YHWH], have done as you pleased" (Jonah 1:14 NIV). I am struck here by the realization that the Holy Spirit has given all human beings a sense of the knowledge of God, but they have suppressed it. As the Apostle Paul wrote in Romans 1:21–23, "Their foolish hearts were darkened. Professing to be wise, they became fools, and changed the glory of the incorruptible God into an image made like to corruptible man—and to birds and four-footed animals and creeping things" (NKJV).

Nevertheless, the seventh-century sailors from Assyria were aware of the presence of YHWH and certainly had a sense of right and wrong. Feeling that their actions were authorized—even commanded—by YHWH, they picked up Jonah and hurled him into the sea. But YHWH was not taken by surprise because He knew in advance what the sailors would do, and He had pre-pared a giant fish to swallow Jonah. (As a point of correction to the prevailing teaching on this story, this was not a whale. It was probably a specially created sea creature with a mouth large enough to swallow a man and a stomach large enough to keep him alive.)

When the storm ceased, the sailors offered sacrifices to YHWH. In the belly of the fish, Jonah prayed, "What I have vowed, I will make good. Salvation comes from the LORD [YHWH]. And the LORD [YHWH] commanded the fish, and it vomited Jonah onto dry land" (Jonah 2:9–10 NIV).

"The word of the LORD [YHWH] came to Jonah a second time: 'Go to the great city of Nineveh and proclaim to it the message that I give you'" (Jonah 3:1–2 NIV). And Jonah obeyed the word of YHWH and went to Nineveh. The power of the message of God's Holy Spirit was so strong in Jonah that as he preached about the judgment of God to fall on Nineveh in forty days, the king of Nineveh and his nobles put on sackcloth and ashes and proclaimed a fast, calling out to YHWH for mercy and forgiveness. Of course, our merciful God saw these people (120,000 of them), withheld judgment, and forgave them for the sins they had committed. But instead of rejoicing that the people had heard his message, repented, and received forgiveness, Jonah was angry because his doomsday prophecy would not be fulfilled.

This should serve as quite a warning to men of the cloth, economists, and politicians who become obsessed with a message of disaster and feel discredited when a gracious God lifts the hand of judgment.

I think the message here is that the Holy Spirit of God is at work among all people and all cultures. When they reject Him, He does not hesitate to bring punishment, but He also waits to pardon and forgive. We read in Hebrews 13:8 that "Jesus Christ is the same yesterday and today and forever" (NIV). The Holy Spirit lives in eternity. He sees the end from the beginning, He plans for the future for His people, He goes before us to prepare the way, and He watches over His word to perform it. He will speak to His servants, and if His servants will utter His word, whole populations can be transformed.

CHAPTER 12

A CORRUPT AND DISSOLUTE NATION

The prophet Amos lived in southern Judah at the same time as Hosea. His message was directed by the Holy Spirit against the northern kingdom two years before an earthquake, when Uzziah was king of Judah and Jeroboam was king of Israel. Amos used this refrain over and over again: "This is what the LORD [YHWH] says.... This is what the LORD [YHWH] says.... This is what the LORD [YHWH] says."

Then Amos trumpeted the sins of Damascus and Aram, the sins of Gaza, then Tyre, Edom, Ammon, Moab, and Judah. According to him, they took captives in battle and disregarded brotherhood. They also ripped open pregnant women, desecrated the bones of a king, and rejected the law of YHWH and did not keep His decrees. YHWH was angry with Judah because the leaders caused the Nazarites to drink wine (in defiance of the vow they had taken before God) and commanded the prophets not to prophesy. However, the Holy Spirit infused Amos's writings with timeless gems, one of which is this: "The Sovereign LORD [YHWH] does nothing without revealing his plans to his servants the prophets" (Amos 3:7 NIV).

The people had ignored the needs of the poor while they feasted on the fat of the land, and even the women had oppressed the poor, crushed the needy, and demanded strong drink from their husbands. Amos showed the concern of the Holy Spirit for social justice, and His revulsion at secular hedonism.

Amos, moved by the Holy Spirit, said, "I hate, I despise your religious festivals. Your assemblies are a stench to me.... Away with the noise of your songs!... Let justice roll on like a river, righteousness like a never-failing stream" (Amos 5:21–25 NIV). Amos, speaking by the Holy Spirit, warns the people not to be at ease in Zion, but to grieve for their sins.

We see through Amos a picture of a corrupt and dissolute nation fat with prosperity, having an abundance of food and drink, lovely homes, and luxurious clothing. Yet they cannot see the coming disaster the day of the Lord might bring, nor do they stir themselves to reach out to the poor and needy to assist them in their suffering. The lament that the Holy Spirit placed in the heart of His prophet, Amos, is not unlike what we read in the book of Revelation about the church at Laodicea, which was proud, filled with goods, and in need of nothing. In short, the Holy Spirit despises religious practice that does not include compassion for the poor or an acknowledgment of pending judgment which may come suddenly, destroying the luxurious life people enjoy.

Without question, the message of Amos reaches across the centuries to our day: those who call themselves Christian but are "at ease in Zion," who do not have compassion for the suffering people in this country and in other nations, and who spend great sums of money on their own religious establishment but have little to give for missions grieve God's heart.

For that matter, think what would happen if just 10 percent of church budgets were spent on missions and another 10 or 20 percent on relief for the poor. Instead, church budgets deal with the salaries of the staff, repairs to the church building, and possible mortgages for newer and grander structures—all without earnest prayer to receive the fullness of God's Spirit and bring about revival throughout the world.

If the Christian Church was really alert, considering we can count among our members at least half the total population of the United States, would we have permitted the abortions of some sixty million precious unborn children? Would we have permitted homosexual marriage? Would we have permitted the homeless to overrun the streets in our major cities? And would we have permitted militant forces to overrun Arab nations near the cradle of Christianity by forcing Christians to deny the deity of Jesus Christ at gunpoint, as ISIS did only a few years ago?

As individual Christians, what part of our personal resources do we spend to take the Gospel of Jesus Christ throughout the world? Just think of the huge amount of money that would be available for missions if all the professing Christians in this nation began to tithe their income to the work of the Lord.

Yet in the midst of judgment, Amos finished with a note of triumph, "'The days are coming,' declares the LORD [YHWH], 'when...I will bring my people Israel back from exile. They will rebuild the ruined cities and live in them. They will plant vineyards and drink their wine; they will make gardens and eat their fruit. I will plant Israel in their own land never again to be uprooted from the land I have given them,' says the LORD [YHWH] your God" (Amos 9:13–15).

CHAPTER 13

WHEN WILL WORLDWIDE PEACE COME?

The prophet Micah was sent by God to speak to the southern kingdom of Judah and the northern kingdom of Samaria during the time of King Hezekiah, who reigned from approximately 715–686 BC. The Holy Spirit placed in Micah's mind a revelation of judgment and collapse, followed by glorious restoration. More particularly, through him the Holy Spirit brought forth one more witness to the authenticity of the life of Jesus Christ when He appeared on Earth.

It was Micah who wrote these words: "But you, Bethlehem Ephrathah, though you are small among the clans of Judah, out of you will come for me one who will be ruler over Israel, whose origins are from of old, from ancient times" (Micah 5:2 NIV).

It was also Micah who spoke of the last days when he wrote,

In the last days the mountain of the LORD's [YHWH's] temple will be established as the highest of the mountains; it will be exalted above the hills, and peoples will stream to it.

Many nations will come and say, "Come, let us go up to the mountain of the LORD [YHWH], to the temple of the God of Jacob. He will teach us his ways, so that we may walk in his paths." The law will go out from Zion, the word of the LORD [YHWH] from Jerusalem. He will judge between many peoples and will settle disputes for strong nations far and wide. They will beat their swords into plowshares and their spears into pruning hooks. Nation will not take up sword against nation, nor will they train for war anymore. Everyone will sit under their own vine and under their own fig tree, and no one will make them afraid, for the LORD [YHWH] Almighty has spoken. All the nations may walk in the name of their gods, but we will walk in the name of the LORD [YHWH] our God forever and ever. (Micah 4:1–5 NIV)

The promise of universal peace has been proclaimed over and over again in the various assemblies of nations. The concept of converting weapons of war into implements of peace brings forth an image which indeed stirs the hearts of men.

However, the Holy Spirit (YHWH) clearly established that universal peace will not take place until the nations submit to the authority of YHWH. He will sit as a benign arbiter of truth, to settle peaceably the disputes which now lead to warfare between the nations. Without question, the Bible makes it clear that universal peace will not come through a United Nations or a "New World Order," but only when the Holy Spirit of God and those who submit to His authority assume charge over the affairs of nations.

At the present time, the prevailing sentiment among nations is "peace through strength." In the United States, we don't hesitate to build aircraft carriers which cost in excess of $12 billion. We don't hesitate long to appropriate billions of dollars for a fleet of supersonic fighter aircraft, each of which costs as much as $150 million. We willingly appropriate a portion of the Defense Department's budget for discretionary spending, which, as of the writing of this book, totaled $633 billion. Can we even comprehend what would happen to our world if expenditures of this magnitude were devoted to agriculture, medicine, reforestation, and infrastructure? If the nations of the world would take the funds they spend on swords and convert them to plowshares, the blessing for the human race would be incalculable. This is indeed the future promised by the Holy Spirit through the words of the prophet Micah.

As an interesting aside, Micah included a warning against the treachery of some of the evil people who lived in his age and time. Jesus Christ directly quoted this prophecy concerning the days following His resurrection: "Do not trust a neighbor; put no confidence in a friend. Even with the woman who lies in your embrace guard the words of your lips. For a son dishonors his father, a daughter rises up against her mother, a daughter-in-law against her mother-in-law—a man's enemies are the members of his own household" (Micah 7:5–6 NIV). These very words literally played out in Nazi Germany and in Communist Russia, when young people were trained to bear witness against their own parents, many of whom were sent to the concentration camps, the gulags, or the executioner.

It seems from reading many of the Old Testament prophets that YHWH was thoroughly disgusted with the religious leaders of those days, even as Jesus Christ was disgusted with the rulers of His day. But hear these words of condemnation by the prophet:

> But as for me, I am filled with power, with the Spirit of the LORD [YHWH], and with justice and might, to declare to Jacob his transgression, to Israel his sin....
>
> Her leaders judge for a bribe, her priests teach for a price, and her prophets tell fortunes for money. Yet they look for the LORD'S [YHWH's] support and say, "Is not the LORD [YHWH] among us? No disaster will come upon us." Therefore because of you, Zion will be plowed like a field, Jerusalem will become a heap of rubble, the temple hill a mound overgrown with thickets. (Micah 3:8, 11–12 NIV)

In 586 BC, Nebuchadnezzar, the king of Babylon, invaded Jerusalem and sacked the Temple. Everything that the nations of Judah and Israel loved and revered was taken away from them. But the disaster did not come before a warning from several of God's prophets.

Today, our task is to listen to the voice of the Holy Spirit and to discern what He is saying. He does nothing without revealing it to His servants, the prophets. So, what do the prophets and the Holy Spirit say? Are earthquakes, famines, plagues, and signs of impending judgment from a righteous God? Will the warnings of the Old Testament prophets be echoed by the Holy Spirit's speaking to us in our modern world?

In the midst of Micah's words of judgment, the Holy Spirit gave through His prophet the formula for what He desired. "The LORD [YHWH] has shown you, O mortal, what is good. And what does the LORD [YHWH] require of you? To act justly and to love mercy and to walk humbly with your God" (Micah 6:8 NIV). In truth, the Holy Spirit who conceived a world of vast complexity has given to humanity very simple commandments: "Love your neighbor as yourself." "Do unto others as you would have them do unto you." "Love the LORD [YHWH] your God with all your heart, soul, and mind, and your neighbor as yourself." "Act justly and love mercy and walk humbly before your God" (my paraphrases). These rules are not complex.

For example, a wayward son might say to his father, "I don't understand what you are saying." And the father might say, "What is it about *no* that you don't understand?" The whole duty of man is to bend his free will to the gracious will of the Triune God—Father, Son, and Holy Spirit.

CHAPTER 14

WHO CAN ENDURE THE DAY
OF HIS COMING?

The last book of the Old Testament, Malachi, means "my
messenger." The Holy Spirit showed Malachi the imminent
coming of the Lord. As a matter of fact, the words of the first
chapter of Malachi are prominently featured in Handel's memorable work *The Messiah*. Malachi wrote that the coming of
YHWH would be like a refiner's fire, and who could stand
before His coming? In this he echoed the words of so many of
the prophets: that the day of YHWH would be a frightful event
which would bring forth judgment.

Think of these words from Malachi 3:2: "Who can endure
the day of his coming? Who can stand when he appears? For He
will be like a refiner's fire or a launderer's soap" (NIV). Then
YHWH will bring before Himself in judgment those who have
oppressed or defrauded others. And He tells us this: "'Surely the
day is coming. It will burn like a furnace. All the arrogant and
every evildoer will be stubble, and the day that is coming will

set them on fire,' says the LORD [YHWH] Almighty. Not a root or a branch will be left to them" (Malachi 4:1 NIV).

We find the same concept in the writings of the Apostle Paul, who said,

> According to the grace of God which was given to me, as a wise master builder I have laid the foundation, and another builds on it. But let each one take heed how he builds on it. For no other foundation can anyone lay than that which is laid, which is Jesus Christ. Now if anyone builds on this foundation with gold, silver, precious stones, wood, hay, straw, each one's work will become clear; for the Day will declare it, because it will be revealed by fire; and the fire will test each one's work, of what sort it is. If anyone's work which he has built on it endures, he will receive a reward. If anyone's work is burned, he will suffer loss; but he himself will be saved, yet so as through fire. (1 Corinthians 3:10–15 NKJV)

Without question, the Holy Spirit brings unity in our concept of the Day of the Lord.

In John 5:24 we learn, "Very truly I tell you, whoever hears my word and believes him who sent Me has eternal life and will not be judged but has crossed over from death to life" (NIV). So those who have received Jesus Christ as their Savior and believe that He is the Son of God will not be judged at the Great White Throne spoken of in the book of Revelation. However, the Apostle Paul tells us that we will, as Christians, stand before the Bema, or judgment seat of Christ, to account for the things that we have done here on Earth. If our works as Christians are self-centered and frivolous, we will still enter into Heaven, but our works will be burned up.

We return now to Malachi, who, having warned us of the terror of the judgment of YHWH, also told us that "those who feared the LORD [YHWH] spoke to one another, and the LORD [YHWH] listened and heard them; so a book of remembrance was written before Him for those who fear the LORD [YHWH] and meditate on His name" (Malachi 3:16 NKJV). And YHWH said, "And you will again see the distinction between the righteous and the wicked, between those who serve God and those who do not" (Malachi 3:18 NIV).

Then once again, Scripture tells us that the day of YHWH will "burn like a furnace" and "all the arrogant and every evil-doer will be stubble, and the day that is coming will set them on fire.... Not a root or a branch will be left of them" (Malachi 4:1 NIV). But on the other hand, those who fear YHWH will leap "with joy like calves let out to pasture" (Malachi 4:2 NLT).

The last words of the Old Testament say, "Look, I am sending you the prophet Elijah.... His preaching will turn the hearts of fathers to their children, and the hearts of children to their fathers. Otherwise, I will come and strike the land with a curse" (Malachi 4:5 NLT). They foretold the coming of a prophet like Elijah, who would bring reconciliation between the young and the old.

Indeed, when Jesus began His ministry, He pointed to John the Baptist as the Elijah who would come to prepare the way of the Lord. The Holy Spirit knit together the prophetic word found in the Old Covenant and that found in the New Covenant.

We are reminded of the Apostle Peter's words to the crowd assembled on the Day of Pentecost when the Holy Spirit was poured out. Quoting from the Book of Joel, he said, "It shall come about after this that I will pour out My Spirit on all mankind; and your sons and daughters will prophesy, your old men will dream dreams, your young men will see visions" (Joel 2:28 AMP).

We now turn our attention to a time when the Holy Spirit was not imparted merely to kings, prophets, and holy men, but to the millions of people who have been born again and spiritually transformed by the Spirit of the Living God.

NEW COVENANT

CHAPTER 15

THE VIRGIN BIRTH

As we attempt to discern the mystery of the Triune God—Father, Son, and Holy Spirit—we must be certain that what is written here corresponds to the total revelation of God presented in the Old and New Testaments. I now want to bring in a unique example of the power of the Holy Spirit.

In Luke 1:26, the angel Gabriel was sent to visit a young girl named Mary who was a virgin (the Greek word *parthenos*.) I want to emphasize the fact that this young girl, betrothed to a man named Joseph, had not engaged in sexual relations with him or with any other man. She was a true virgin. The angel said, "You will conceive in your womb and give birth to a son, and you shall name Him Jesus" (Luke 1:31 NASB). And Mary's quick response was, "How will this be, since I am a virgin?" The angel replied, "The Holy Spirit will come upon you, and the power of the Most High will overshadow you; for that reason also the holy Child will be called the Son of God" (Luke 1:34–35 NASB).

Later on we learn that Joseph, when he discovered that his fiancé was pregnant, decided to put her away quietly, because in that society pregnancy outside of marriage could have led to a stoning. Before Joseph could carry out his intention, an angel appeared to him and said, "Fear not to take unto thee Mary thy wife: for that which is conceived in her is of the Holy Ghost" (Matthew 1:20 KJV).

In today's world, people can use a site called Ancestry.com to earnestly seek out their roots—what nationality they have or their lineage. Mary was of the house and lineage of David, as was Joseph, but Joseph was not the birth father of Jesus. Although this is true, there is no mention of the fact that the true birth father of Jesus was the Holy Spirit. Joseph was never referred to as "father," and for that matter, we don't find much about him after the birth of Jesus. This is somewhat surprising, because later on in the gospels we realize that Joseph was also a descendant of David. After visiting the Temple as a child, Jesus went home with him and Mary and was "obedient to them" (Luke 2:51 NIV). But consider the prayers and attitude of Jesus after He began His ministry. For example, consider His words in Luke 12:51–52: "Do you think I came to bring peace on earth? No, I tell you, but division. From now on there will be five in one family divided against each other" (NIV). We also learn that Jesus had other half-brothers and half-sisters. But again, these origins are somewhat cloaked in mystery.

As we move forward to what is called the "High Priestly Prayer" of Jesus Christ in John 17, He prayed to His Father and said, "Father, the hour has come. Glorify your Son that your Son may glorify you.... Now, Father, glorify me in your presence with the glory I had with you before the world began" (John 17:1, 5 NIV). Keep in mind that neither Joseph nor Mary had ever been with the Father before the earth was made. How could the man Jesus say that He who had been born of Mary was indeed with the Father before the earth began? He told His disciples that He was returning to the Father, but how could it be that this man who lived among the people of Israel came from the Father? And yet, that is what the record shows. If the Holy Spirit came upon a virgin and implanted a seed in her womb, how could that seed have grown to the point where Jesus felt He had come from the Father and was returning to the Father? And why would Jesus not acknowledge the cause of His birth as the Holy Spirit, not God the Father?

Yet He told His disciples before His ascension that He was going to His Father and to their Father. The model prayer begins, "Our Father which art in Heaven, hallowed be thy name" (Matthew 6:9 KJV).

And the young Jesus at age twelve was found in the temple speaking to the elders and showing incredible wisdom. When rebuked by His earthly parents, Mary and Joseph, He said, "Did you not know that I must be about My Father's business?" (Luke 2:49 NKJV).

We learn also that when Jesus was with His disciples, "Philip said to Him, 'Lord, show us the Father and it is sufficient for us.'" And Jesus replied, 'He who has seen Me has seen the Father'" (John 14:8–9 NKJV). Here again, we have the mystery of the Trinity of God. The Holy Spirit implanted a seed in Mary, and that seed became the Son of God, who prayed to the Head of the Trinity to give Him the glory that He had with the Father before the foundation of the earth. Yet He told His disciples that if they had seen Him, they had seen the Father.

Once, when challenged about His origins, He said, "Before Abraham was born, *I am*" (John 8:58 NIV). And remember the burning bush when Moses asked who was speaking to him. The reply was, "*I AM THAT I AM*" (Exodus 3:14 KJV). Here, Jesus Christ identified Himself with the Triune God. In Revelation 5 the worship of the multitudes was directed "unto him who sitteth upon the throne, and unto the Lamb for ever and ever" (Revelation 5:13 KJV). Why would the man Jesus on Earth speak of the Head of the Trinity as Father and not in any way acknowledge that the Holy Spirit brought Him life on Earth?

When we pray, we pray to the Father, "In the name of Jesus and with the power of the Holy Spirit." I want to ensure that in this book we have been faithful to the scriptural account and, at the same time, have not done violence to the mystery of the Triune God. I asked personally for revelation and understanding of how His nature works, and I hope that this book has helped enlighten you to one of the great mysteries of the universe. But suffice it to say that as we see the practical outworking of the Holy Spirit in the lives of Christian believers, the power of God becomes abundantly manifest.

CHAPTER 16

THE POWER OF PENTECOST

In what is called the High Priestly Prayer, in which Jesus brought His disciples into the extraordinary intimacy He had with His Father, He told them:

> It is for your good that I am going away. Unless I go away, the Advocate will not come to you; but if I go, I will send him to you. When he comes, he will prove the world to be in the wrong about sin and righteousness and judgment...about judgment, because the prince of this world now stands condemned.
>
> I have much more to say to you, more than you can now bear. But when he, the Spirit of truth, comes, he will guide you into all the truth. He will not speak on his own; he will speak only what he hears, and he will

tell you what is yet to come. He will glorify me because it is from me that he will receive what he will make known to you. (John 16:7–14 NIV)

After the resurrection, Jesus Christ in His risen form appeared to His disciples, who were locked in an Upper Room for fear of the Jews. He then commissioned them with these words: "As the Father has sent me, I am sending you." And with that, He breathed on them and said, "Receive the Holy Spirit. If you forgive anyone's sins, they are forgiven; if you do not forgive them, they are not forgiven" (John 20:21–23 NIV).

In the book of Acts, before Jesus was taken up into Heaven, He said to them, "Do not leave Jerusalem, but wait for the gift my Father promised, which you have heard me speak about. For John baptized with water, but in a few days you will be baptized with the Holy Spirit" (Acts 1:4–5 NIV). Then He said to them, "It is not for you to know the times or dates the Father has set in his own authority. But you will receive power when the Holy Spirit comes on you; and you will be my witnesses in Jerusalem, and in all Judea and Samaria, and to the ends of the earth" (Acts 1:7–8 NIV).

The Feast of Pentecost came fifty days after the Passover. We know Jesus was offered as the sacrifice on the cross over the Passover weekend. After the Passover in Jewish tradition, the Feast of First Fruits or Pentecost was celebrated. When the Day of Pentecost came and the disciples were sitting in an upper room, the Holy Spirit descended on them in power. They were baptized in the Holy Spirit and became the first fruits of the new Christian faith which, under the power of the Holy Spirit, has spread throughout the earth and become the largest religious faith in the world with 2.6 billion adherents.

Under the power of the Holy Spirit, those people who were praying in one accord in the Upper Room burst out into the streets of Jerusalem. The Spirit of God put into their minds the languages of the multitudes of people who had come from all over the Roman Empire to celebrate a particular Jewish festival in Jerusalem. The assembled people were astounded when they heard simple Galileans speaking the languages of the Medes and Parthians, as well as people from Mesopotamia, Cappadocia, Egypt, Libya, Rome itself, and other parts of the Mediterranean world. These people were not "preaching the Gospel." They were declaring under the power of the Holy Spirit the "wonders of God." Some said, "These are simple Galileans. Where did they learn these languages?" Others, scoffing, said, "This is nothing but drunken babbling" (see Acts 2, my paraphrases).

The Apostle Peter stood up in their midst and said,

> These people are not drunk as you suppose. It's only nine in the morning! No, this is what was spoken by the prophet Joel:
> "In the last days, God says, I will pour out my Spirit on all people. Your sons and daughters will prophesy, your young men will see visions, your old men will dream dreams. Even on my servants, both men and women, I will pour out my Spirit in those days, and they will prophesy.... And everyone who calls on the name of the LORD will be saved." (Acts 2:15–18, 21 NIV)

If indeed "He who causes everything to be," or YHWH, is the Holy Spirit, then some might ask, "Why didn't the prophet say, 'I will pour Myself upon all flesh'?" But the Bible is very clear in distinguishing the functions of the various members of the Trinity. The Father is the Creative Mind, the Son is the expression of the Father, and the Holy Spirit is the link with creation. In no way would the Scriptures ignore the separate functions of each member of the Holy Trinity. It is God the Father who pours out the Holy Spirit upon all flesh, giving believers supernatural utterance to declare the manifold wonders of God.

Peter went on to say, "God has raised this Jesus to life, and we are all witnesses of it. Exalted to the right hand of God, he has received from the Father the promised Holy Spirit and has poured out what you now see and hear" (Acts 2:32–33 NIV).

Then the people cried out to Peter and said, "'What shall we do?' Peter replied, 'Repent and be baptized, every one of you, in the name of Jesus Christ for the forgiveness of your sins. And you will receive the gift of the Holy Spirit. The promise is for you and your children and for all who are far off—for all whom the Lord our God will call'" (Acts 2:38–39 NIV).

Here was the promise of the gift of the Holy Spirit to all who believe in Jesus Christ. No longer was the Spirit limited to holy men and select leaders. All who believed in Jesus were candidates to receive this blessed gift from God Almighty, promised by the prophet Joel and demonstrated on the day of Pentecost by the Holy Spirit Himself.

Some people have wondered about the difference between being born again by the Holy Spirit and being baptized in the

Holy Spirit. Did the disciples not receive the Holy Spirit when Jesus breathed upon them? Of course they did. Unless a person has been born again by the Spirit of God, he is not part of the family of God. Had the disciples become "Christians" when Jesus breathed upon them and told them to receive the Holy Spirit? Of course they had. Why, then, did Jesus ask His disciples to wait for the promise of the Father for their baptism in the Holy Spirit? What is the difference?

Let me illustrate. As I am writing this book, I am drinking water. It can clearly be said that I have water in me. That is like the salvation experience, when we receive the Spirit of God in our hearts. However, sixteen miles from where I am sitting is the shore of the Atlantic Ocean, which connects to all the oceans on the earth. If I drive to the Virginia Beach seashore and dive into the water, I am now immersed in a massive flood which overwhelms my entire body. Obviously, I am connected to water either way, but the second experience is thousands of times more dramatic. So was the experience of these humble fishermen when the power of the Holy Spirit came upon them on the Day of Pentecost. Yes, the disciples had within them the power of the Spirit, but until the Day of Pentecost they did not have the power of the baptism of the Spirit, which would enable them to go forth from Jerusalem and one day conquer the world.

Now let us look at the effect of the indwelling Spirit in the life of a believer, and then the effect of the baptism of this Spirit upon the life of the same believer.

When the Holy Spirit comes into a person's life, He begins to bring forth in that person the attitudes that we consider Christlike. These are called the fruits of the Spirit. The chief elements of the fruits of the Spirit are three-fold: faith, hope, and love. In the thirteenth chapter of Paul's first letter to the church at Corinth, he gave a verbal portrait of the essential characteristics of Jesus Christ when he spoke of love.

> Love is patient, love is kind. It does not envy, it does not boast, it is not proud. It does not dishonor others, it is not self-seeking, it is not easily angered, it keeps no record of wrongs. Love does not delight in evil but rejoices in the truth. It always protects, always trusts, always hopes, always perseveres. Love never fails. (1 Corinthians 13:4–8 NIV)

In his letter to the Romans, the Apostle Paul showed how the fruit of the Holy Spirit is developed in our life when he told us, "The testing of our faith produces endurance" (James 1:3 NASB). The Greek language can be very expressive, and in some cases the words have a sound which reflect the meaning. We call that onomatopoeia. The Greek word for endurance is *hupomone*, in which you can almost hear the groaning and suffering of someone under a large burden. By faith, when the fruit of the Spirit is placed under stress and survives it, character is produced; the person so tried begins to show qualities of stability and resilience not unlike iron, which is strengthened by fire. With character, the individual so tested realizes that he or she overcame great difficulties and then realizes, like Job, that the Redeemer lives—and therefore, he or she can hope in Him.

We are told, "Hope maketh not ashamed; because the love of God is shed abroad in our hearts" (Romans 5:5 KJV). When we truly hope in God, we are able to forget about ourselves. We put all the cares of this life aside and focus our attention on the needs of others. When we truly hope in God, we are free to love God and love our fellow man. With hope, the Holy Spirit begins manifesting the grace of Jesus Christ in us—the same grace that Jesus Christ experienced when He died to demonstrate the love of the Father for the world.

After physical death when our bodies cease to exist, our Spirits will live on in Heaven. The fruit of the Holy Spirit (faith, hope, and love) will go with us for all eternity.

CHAPTER 17

THE OUTPOURED SPIRIT

I f the indwelling Spirit produces the beautiful fruit of the Spirit, what does the outpoured Spirit produce? An amazing array of spiritual enablements. The word *charis* in Greek means "grace," and the enablements of the Holy Spirit which reproduce the miracle works of Jesus are called *charismata*, or "grace gifts."

There are times when a Christian baptized in the Holy Spirit will receive a special anointing for power to accomplish an extraordinary task. At such times, the Holy Spirit, who has all power, can come upon one of His servants who has been baptized in Him to give him or her a special filling which transcends the norm. This means that believers can experience one baptism of the Holy Spirit, and also many fillings of the Spirit which cause them to rise under extraordinary circumstances.

The *charismata* are divided into three principal categories: those of utterance, those of revelation, and those of power. The

Holy Spirit can manifest Himself in utterance by providing the ability to speak in tongues, to interpret those tongues, and to speak in prophecy. Prophecy in this context does not mean telling the future, but giving words from God to the Church for edification, exhortation, and comfort. The Apostle Paul said that "he who speaks in an unknown tongue edifies himself" (1 Corinthians 14:4 MEV). In other words, it is to build up one's own spirit. In the assembly of believers, the interpretation of the message in tongues is equivalent to prophecy for edification, exhortation, and comfort.

The manifestations of revelation include the word of knowledge, which is a revelation by the Holy Spirit of something not available to the senses. This is not some psychic manifestation, but a clear word to a believer of something that is happening and not readily available to the five senses. It is also slightly different from a word of wisdom, which is more complex.

King Solomon possessed what we know as wisdom. He had a vast knowledge of the physical world and an acute sense of right and wrong. He showed this dramatically when he discerned which of two competing women was the true mother of a baby they both claimed as their own. The ability to order our affairs with wisdom should be highly prized by all believers. In my personal prayer life there is an almost daily request to receive from God wisdom, favor, and anointing.

However, a word of wisdom is something different. Wisdom is a blessing that God gives to His people to enable them to order their affairs and deal intelligently with the world around them. A word of wisdom deals with future occurrences not available to the recipient except through the Holy Spirit. If coupled with prophecy, it can become a directive from God about future events, but to my understanding this is a rare occurrence.

The other revelatory enablement of the outpouring is called the discernment of spirits. This is not discerning demons; it is a perception of the invisible world that lies beyond the visible. But it also gives the one who possesses it the ability to see the real spiritual nature of some people. Every human being has some kind of façade. It's what we see on the outside. Inside of some people is a pure heart and a gentle spirit. Inside of other people is an evil heart and an impure spirit. To a person who possesses discernment of spirits, what lies behind the mask becomes obvious.

Beyond human reality there also lies a spiritual world of angels and demons. Seeing the spiritual nature that underlies the activity of an organization, a city, a state, or a nation can be invaluable. But it also can be terrifying. This is a type of knowledge that many Christians are not mature enough to handle successfully.

Remember the time when Philip brought Nathanael to Jesus and Jesus remarked, "Behold an Israelite indeed, in whom is no guile!" (John 1:47 KJV). Jesus saw the beauty of Nathanael's spirit, and Nathanael was amazed: "How did you know me, Lord?" (John 1:48 NIV). With Nathanael, discernment of spirits was a pleasant experience. But looking into the spirit behind a deranged lunatic like Charles Manson would have been terrifying for most people.

Remember the story of the prophet Elisha? When confronted by an army intent on capturing him, he remarked to his servant, "Those who are with us are greater than those who are with them" (2 Kings 6:16 NASB). By exercising his discernment gift, Elisha and his servant saw the hills surrounded by angelic beings sent to protect them from the king of Aram.

This enablement of the Holy Spirit is a superb way for a counselor to develop empathy with a client or patient. For many years, mental health professionals viewed religious faith as a type of sickness, but now more and more they are realizing the value of spiritual understanding in dealing with those who are grieving, fearful, troubled, or psychotic.

The other of the nine *charismata* are the manifestations of power, which include healing, miracles, and faith. I believe I am correct in saying that though Spirit-filled Christians throughout the ages have had very dramatic ministries of healing, no one has been given a gift to heal. If an individual had a gift to heal, he or she could go through a hospital and heal every sick person in it. A healing under the power of the Holy Spirit involves an acceleration of a process already begun or the removal of a malign force, physical or spiritual, which has created an illness. With prayer, under the authority of the Holy Spirit, a process takes place which brings forth wholeness to a person and the removal of the pathogen or malignant force that caused the illness.

In my own life, I have seen blind people receive their sight, the deaf receive their hearing, people with cancer made whole, and sufferers of multiple sclerosis stand up and push wheelchairs out of a meeting hall. But in each instance these healings were a manifestation of the Holy Spirit, and it would be the wildest flight of fancy for me to claim I have a "gift of healing."

A miracle normally implies a creative act. For example, a blind person receives a new eyeball. A man missing a leg has a new leg grow out. A woman with no reproductive organs becomes pregnant and bears a child. Miraculous things like this take place all around the world in this day, even as they took place in the days of the disciples of Jesus after the out-pouring of Pentecost.

Finally, faith is granted as a working of power. Jesus told His disciples that if they had faith as small as a mustard seed, they could speak to the Mount of Olives and command it to fall into the Dead Sea, and it would obey them. There are times in the Christian's life when he or she is absolutely overwhelmed with a task at hand, and yet the Holy Spirit brings supernatural faith. Suddenly, what seems impossible yields to a commanding word from the Holy Spirit through an individual's demonstrating this faith. As Scripture tells us, "If two of you on earth agree about anything they ask for, it will be done for them by my Father in heaven" (Matthew 18:19 NIV).

I have several personal examples of this. When I finished seminary, I was praying about God's direction for my life. I had been challenged by a high school friend to claim a television station in Tidewater, Virginia, for the glory of the Lord. I had little or no money. I did not own a television set. I knew abso-lutely nothing about operating a television station. Yet one day when a former classmate from seminary asked me what I was going to do next, the power of faith burst forth in my voice and I said with absolute assurance, "I am going to Virginia to start a television station." This was faith in action, and indeed it came to pass. I also saw faith rise in my heart.

Later, a hurricane was hurtling through the Atlantic, threat-ening to destroy our fledgling ministry. When I asked participants at a prayer breakfast in a hotel in Norfolk, Virginia, to point their hands toward the storm and pray, the power of the Holy Spirit brought forth supernatural faith, and without hesitation, I commanded that mighty storm to move away from our area and turn back to where it came from. Indeed, the storm responded not to me, but to the faith given by the Holy Spirit of God. Despite the derision I received on account of this, the track of that hurricane still on record bears witness to the reality of the Holy Spirit's power given to His servants today.

CHAPTER 18

LED BY THE SPIRIT OF GOD

Among the greatest blessings that the Holy Spirit can give to His servants is ongoing direction for their lives. How does He do it? The Bible tells us, "For as many as are led by the Spirit of God, they are the sons of God" (Romans 8:14 KJV). It also says, "Your ears shall hear a word behind you, saying, 'This is the way, walk in it,' whenever you turn to the right hand or whenever you turn to the left" (Isaiah 30:21 NKJV).

In remembering the story of Elijah in the Old Testament, YHWH appeared to him not in a rock-crushing hurricane or a turbulent storm, but in a still, small voice. The Bible tells us, "Be still, and know that I am God" (Psalm 46:10 NIV). I believe that if we are quiet before the Holy Spirit, He will quietly speak to us and give us directions. We have an absolute right as children to approach our Father and to ask Him for directions.

In my public life, I was laughed at by saying that God had directed me to do certain things. I replied, "Of course God directs me. Can you imagine an employee who worked for thirty years for a corporation and never once heard a word from his boss?" Of course God guides us, and if we will be quiet and listen, the Holy Spirit directs us in the way that we should go. Since the Holy Spirit is within us, His peace will rest upon us quietly while we are going about our day-to-day affairs. However, if we undertake a relationship, a business venture, a journey, or any enterprise and suddenly find that our spirits within us are troubled, we may realize that the umpire has warned us that our course is either dangerous for us or not in the perfect will of the Holy Spirit.

The Apostle Paul wrote that we should "always pray without ceasing" (1 Thessalonians 5:17 NKJV). I personally make it my habit to talk to God all the time. This is the communion that Adam had with His Creator in the Garden of Eden before the Fall. This is the communion that Jesus Christ died to bring to His people after His death and resurrection. He said, "My Father has not left Me alone, for I always do what pleases Him" (John 8:29 AMPC). As His servants, we cry out to Him, "Lord, make me part of Your plan. What would You have me to do? What do You plan for this nation?"

Of course, beyond the day-to-day talk in prayer with the Lord, every believer should set aside a time when he or she can be alone to read the Bible, pray, meditate on the things of God, and ask Him for direction. I am absolutely convinced that God will not allow one of His servants to be misled if that servant earnestly asks Him for direction.

Remember how Jesus said, "If a son asks for bread from any father among you, will he give him a stone? Or if he asks for a fish, will he give him a serpent instead of a fish?" (Luke 11:11 NKJV). And then He said, "If you then, being evil, know how to give good gifts to your children, how much more will your heavenly Father give the Holy Spirit to those who ask Him?" (Luke 11:13 NKJV). I would venture to say that if half of the Christians in America were asked what they had prayed for that particular morning, they would not have an answer. I believe we should be precise. We should come before the Lord during a quiet time and enter into His presence with thanksgiving. Then with prayer and supplication we should make our requests known to God (Philippians 4:7). I believe it's important that we know what we are asking of God; then He will receive glory when He gives us the answer. Jesus said it so well: "Hitherto have ye asked nothing in my name: ask, and ye shall receive, that your joy may be full" (John 16:24 KJV). Keep in mind as you pray that your heavenly Father delights to give good gifts to His children. He will not give you something which will bring harm to you, but those things that bring joy to your life will be freely given. *"Ask and you shall receive"* (Matthew 7:7, paraphrase and emphasis mine).

However, beyond our asking the Bible tells us that the Father knows exactly what our needs are. In fact, the Holy Spirit groans within us. He knows what is in our spirit and responds accordingly.

We are told clearly not to be anxious about what we should eat or what we should drink or what we should wear because "your Father knows that you need these things" (Luke 12:30 NKJV). Instead, we are to "seek first the kingdom of God and His righteousness, and all these things shall be added to you"

(Matthew 6:33 NKJV). Jesus told His disciples, "Fear not, little flock; for it is your Father's good pleasure to give you the kingdom" (Luke 12:32 KJV).

Do you see the confidence of a person walking in the Holy Spirit? In Psalm 91, the Lord said, "Because he has set his love upon Me, therefore, I will…" (verse 14 NKJV). He then went forth to announce protection, provision, honor, long life, and the revelation of God's nature—all because he set his love upon Him.

Perhaps my favorite chapter in the Bible is Romans 8, which declares, "We are more than conquerors through Him who loved us" (Romans 8:37 NKJV). Isaiah tells us, "No weapon formed against you will prosper.… This is the heritage of the servants of the LORD [YHWH]" (Isaiah 54:17 NKJV).

Our life under the power of the Holy Spirit should be one of complete victory. The Holy Spirit will energize the words of His children, and "a man's stomach shall be satisfied from the fruit of his mouth" (Proverbs 18:20 NKJV). Remember that we partake of the image of God. Therefore, His word in our mouth will have power even as His word in His mouth. We must always be careful to ensure that our words become a blessing to us and those around us. We must guard against saying those things which will actually destroy the prospects that lie before us. If we profess good, good will come to us, because we have in our mouth the power to create an environment of blessing for us and our family. However, that same power when used negatively can lead us into continuous despair, poverty, and failure. This isn't some hocus-pocus mind over matter; this is basic spiritual reality.

Remember also that the devil earnestly desires worship. He envies the Creator who is freely worshiped by His creation. The devil wants to steal that worship, and he will take it any way he can get it. If we give the devil credit for things that happen in our lives, he welcomes this as worship. He even welcomes curses in his name. We should be totally repulsed by well-meaning Christians who say things like, "The devil made me do it." The Bible tells us to never "give place to the devil" (Ephesians 4:27 KJV).

Under the power of the Holy Spirit, we are not to give voice to our fears of demonic influences, disease, poverty, family breakup, or failure. "We are more than conquerors to Him who loved us!" (Romans 8:37 NKJV). Our destiny is to be led "from one degree of glory to another, which is from the Lord, who is the Spirit" (2 Corinthians 3:18 NET).

CHAPTER 19

A MIRACLE OF MULTIPLICATION

When Jesus walked the face of the earth, He and His disciples spent time in a desert place, and a multitude followed Him to hear His teaching. After a couple of days, the crowd began to faint from hunger. The disciples told Jesus of their plight. Instead of providing for the crowd's needs, He told His disciples, "You feed them!" (Matthew 14:16 NLT). Of course, they didn't have enough money to buy food, and even if they had, it was unlikely that any store was available with adequate supplies for five thousand people. You can imagine the disciples' shock when Jesus told them to bring to Him what they had. As they searched around, they found a little boy who had brought his meager lunch from home—five small loaves of pita bread and two little fish.

Jesus knew what He was going to do, but His disciples had no clue. He said, "Have them sit down in groups" (Luke 9:14 NIV). Then He took the few loaves and small fish and breathed a blessing upon them. He handed them to His disciples with instructions to begin to feed the people. Somewhere in the process, a miracle of multiplication took place. I like to think it was in the hands of the disciples themselves when they began to break off pieces of the bread and fish and give them to the people. As they did, the bread and fish multiplied so that every single person in that crowd had enough to eat. When they had finished, Jesus ordered the disciples to pick up the leftovers. They were amazed that there were twelve baskets full of bread and fish.

The Holy Spirit is obviously in charge of all material things, and it's nothing to Him to breathe a word and multiply material supplies. God, through His Holy Spirit, can multiply a farmer's crops, a merchant's sales, a stockbroker's profits, and a businessman's customers. Why, then, should we worry, when we have a Father who knows exactly what we need and actually has the answer ready before we even call for it? The Spirit of God is not impressed with the earthly resources of any human being, however rich he or she may be, because the gold and silver are His, as well as the cattle on a thousand hills. And we must all acknowledge that we can give Him nothing except some of what He has already given us.

But what about in our current day? Does God multiply in answer to the prayer of His servants? Let me give you this marvelous example.

The mother of my friend Frank Foglio was a little Pentecostal woman from Italy who had an incredible faith in God. She would take the Scripture, point her finger to it, then lift it up to Heaven and scream, "Hey, God! This is what You promised!" And this dear little lady absolutely expected an answer. One day, her family came home with guests, expecting a meal. But Mama Foglio only had half a box of spaghetti in her cupboard. There was not enough food to feed one family, much less a whole house full of guests. But this fact did not deter Mama Foglio. She took a pot of water, put the few strands of spaghetti in it, then opened the Bible to the passage about Jesus feeding the loaves and the fishes. She held up the Bible, put her finger on the verse, and screamed out, "Hey, God! Help me feed this group of people. I am believing You for the answer."

Then the miracle began to happen. The few strands of spaghetti began to swell, and the pot was filled. She took that spaghetti out and filled up another pot with equally satisfying results. She set the miracle spaghetti in front of her guests, and all the crowd of people had their complete fill of a delicious dinner.

The Bible tells us that Abraham had not sired a child with his beloved wife, Sarah, but YHWH had promised him children as numerous as the sands on the sea. Abraham "amened YHWH," and "he [YHWH] counted it to him as righteousness" (Genesis 15:6 ESV). Hebrews 11:6 tells us that those who come to God "must believe that He is, and that He is a rewarder of those that diligently seek Him" (NKJV).

Under the power of the Holy Spirit, all things are possible. The only impossibility is that God Almighty would deny Himself. As Spirit-filled Christians, we are to be an army in the service of the Holy Spirit—more than conquerors through Him that loved us!

CHAPTER 20

A MIRACLE AT THE GATE BEAUTIFUL

When Jesus Christ told His disciples that they would be baptized in the Holy Spirit, He said, "And ye shall be witnesses unto me both in Jerusalem, and in all Judaea, and in Samaria, and unto the uttermost part of the earth" (Acts 1:8 KJV). What follows next in the biblical account is the expansion of the Christian Church under the power of the baptism of the Holy Spirit.

First, in Jerusalem a small band of Christian believers, despite the initial outpouring of God's Spirit at Pentecost, still faced incredible hostility from the religious leaders of their nation. Without doubt, the religious leaders felt guilty about their part in the crucifixion of One who claimed to be the Messiah. Blame went back and forth throughout the centuries. Were the Romans responsible for the crucifixion of the Messiah, or were the Jewish leaders responsible, or was the nation of Israel itself guilty? Whatever the answer to these questions, the religious leaders did not want the early apostles to stand on the Temple Mount and persuade people that the Jesus they crucified was indeed the Messiah and that they were responsible for his death.

However, the Holy Spirit had no intention of remaining silent to please the rebellious religious leaders. One day, the apostles Peter and John went up to the Temple at the time of prayer, about three o'clock in the afternoon. At that time, they came across a man crippled from birth who was begging for alms. Peter looked at him and under the power of the Holy Spirit said, "Silver or gold I do not have, but what I do have I give you: In the name of Jesus Christ of Nazareth, rise up and walk!" (Acts 3:6 NKJV). Then he took the man by the hand, and as the spirit of faith rose in the crippled man to meet Peter's faith, his feet and ankles were strengthened. He arose and began leaping and dancing and praising God.

As crowds gathered to behold the miracle, Peter preached to the assembled multitude and condemned the religious leaders for the role they played in killing the Son of God. Peter, the fisherman, was now ordering the rabbis and learned scholars of the Law: "Repent...and turn to God, so that your sins may be wiped out, that times of refreshing may come from the Lord" (Acts 3:19 NIV). He then declared that Jesus Christ was in Heaven with the Father and would come again in fulfillment of the prophecy given to the Jews through Moses. In Act 3:26, Peter instructed them in Jesus Christ's command to turn from their wicked ways.

We can only imagine how the lecture of an unlearned fisherman angered these people. But God gave that fisherman the power of the Holy Spirit to bring about complete healing to a man lame from birth. So how could they silence his message?

Peter and John possessed spiritual power, but the religious leaders possessed secular power. They used their power to order the soldiers to seize Peter and John and put them in jail.

On the next day, the High Priest Caiaphas and other men of his family brought Peter and John before them to answer this question: "By what power or what name did you do this?" (Acts 4:7 NIV). In answer to the leaders' questions, Peter, filled with the Holy Spirit, said, "It is by the name of Jesus Christ of Nazareth, whom you crucified but whom God raised from the dead, that this man stands before you healed. Jesus is 'the stone you builders rejected, which has become the cornerstone.' Salvation is found in no one else, for there is no other name under heaven given to mankind by which we must be saved" (Acts 4:10–12 NIV).

The leaders were faced with a dilemma. The whole city realized that the disciples had performed a notable miracle. Yet the leaders also realized that if the multitude accepted the message of the risen Christ, they would lose their ruling position and be kicked out of office. Like a modern-day judge, they issued a gag order forbidding these apostles from speaking any more about the authenticity of Jesus's resurrection and His miraculous power.

At that time, Peter gave a message which should encourage any God-fearing person who wishes to speak out against a tyrannical gag order. Peter and John replied, "Which is right in God's eyes: to listen to you, or to him? You be the judges! As for us, we cannot help speaking about what we have seen and heard" (Acts 4:19–20 NIV).

Peter and John were released from custody and went to the assembled church, then engaged in one of the most memorable prayer meetings in history. They prayed in unison. Once again, we must remember that the disciples were "all with one accord in one place" (Acts 2:1 KJV) when the Holy Spirit came on the Day of Pentecost.

At the time of the Tower of Babel, YHWH said this about human endeavor: "If as one people speaking the same language they have begun to do this, then nothing they plan to do will be impossible for them" (Genesis 11:6 NIV). Jesus told His disciples, "If two of you shall agree on earth as touching anything that they shall ask, it shall be done for them of my Father which is in heaven" (Matthew 18:19 KJV).

I cannot emphasize strongly enough how important it is for Christian believers to agree with one another when they pray. Husbands and wives must agree together in prayer. Parents and children must agree together. If there is discord in a home concerning child-rearing, finances, or work and leisure, there will be friction and lack of power. We need to learn over and over again the clear words of Jesus: "Every kingdom divided against itself is laid waste; and no city or house divided against itself will stand" (Matthew 12:25 NASB).

For the last half century, radical elements have attempted to subvert our democratic form of life. They do so by discrediting our heroes and turning the American people against the foundational principles that have brought success and harmony to this great nation. If the intellectual leaders of our nation turn against the spiritual foundations which have brought forth the greatness of our land, our country ultimately will fall. They accomplish the undermining of these foundations in many subtle ways. Classes turn against classes, the older turn against youth, and youth turn against the older. People of color turn against the white race, immigrants turn against the native-born, and vice versa. Those who have brought prosperity through our capitalistic system are derided as exploiters. The whole purpose of these nefarious exercises is to destroy the United States of America, which—to my way of thinking—is the only nation in the world that can resist tyranny and guarantee democratic freedom.

I have personally made it my goal to bring about harmony among the denominations—especially the relations between Catholics and Protestants. When we are together, nothing is impossible. If we are divided, nothing is possible.

We turn now to this marvelous prayer meeting where the early Christians with one voice cried out to YHWH:

> You made the heavens and the earth and the sea, and everything in them. You spoke by the Holy Spirit through the mouth of your servant, our father David....
>
> They did what your power and will had decided beforehand should happen. Now, Lord, consider their threats and enable your servants to speak your word with great boldness. Stretch out your hand to heal and perform signs and wonders through the name of your holy servant Jesus. (Acts 4:24–25, 28–30 NIV)

The Holy Spirit answered their prayer in power. The place where they met was shaken, and each one of these participants was filled with the Holy Spirit and spoke the Word of God boldly.

Here we learn an important principle. Every one of these believers had been baptized in the Holy Spirit. Every one of them had been born again by the indwelling of the Holy Spirit. Yet in this time of crisis, we are told that they were "filled" with the Holy Spirit. The principle is clear—there is one salvation and one baptism of the Holy Spirit, but there are many fillings, especially when the time comes for extraordinary action by God's people. That is why it is absolutely appropriate—in fact essential—that those of us who know God be equipped with an extra infusion of Holy Spirit power when we face overwhelming challenges in our lives.

I think this is especially true when we have major decisions to make in our lives. It takes little special guidance to get into our car in the morning and drive to work. Of course, at that moment we still should check with the Holy Spirit as to whether the route we choose is appropriate to the activity He has for us for the day. It takes very little guidance from the Holy Spirit to get up from bed and get dressed for the day. It takes little special guidance to eat dinner or go to bed.

But what if we suffer a stroke or develop cancer? What if our child is arrested for drug possession? What if we are offered a promotion at our place of employment which would entail moving to another city? What if we are a single person contemplating marriage? In those instances, big decisions call for big guidance. We need a special anointing of the Holy Spirit before we move ahead. In the next chapter, I will give some examples of ways in which the Holy Spirit can speak to His children with "big guidance."

CHAPTER 21

SUPERNATURAL GUIDANCE DAY BY DAY

O ne of the wonderful benefits of baptism in the Holy Spirit is receiving supernatural guidance on a day-to-day basis from Him. The Apostle Paul directed us to "pray in the Spirit on all occasions with all kinds of prayers and requests. With this in mind, be alert and always keep on praying for all the Lord's people" (Ephesians 6:18 NIV). What a beautiful image this gives. We are walking every day with the Holy Spirit and talking to Him every moment, and He is, in turn, talking to us.

In each one of us, there is a spirit, and when our spirit joins with the Holy Spirit, the deepest part of our emotional being—the heart—is at peace. When we begin a course of action contrary to the will of the Holy Spirit, that peace will lift, and disquietude or trouble will take its place. Scripture says that if we regard iniquity in our hearts, the Lord won't hear us. As we pray in the Holy Spirit, if we are conscious of committing acts of sin against the Lord, our spirit is unable to have peace or to agree with the Holy Spirit. Therefore, our prayers don't get answered. But if we are sensitive to the Holy Spirit's leading, we can call upon Him for direct guidance and answers for the direction that we should take in our lives.

I would like to give you one example from my personal life. Over the years, my wife and I have prayed together often to receive guidance on major issues that confronted us. When we do this, I take my Bible, and Dede takes her Bible, and we both get quiet before the Lord. We ask the Holy Spirit to speak to our minds a verse of Scripture that will answer the question before us. I pray and wait on the Lord, and Dede prays and waits on the Lord. The Holy Spirit gives each one of us verses in the Bible, and we share with one another what God has told us.

One time when we did this, a dramatic occurrence took place concerning a television station in southern Lebanon. For years I had attempted to obtain a broadcast license that would enable CBN to broadcast the Gospel to the Middle East, especially to Israel. All doors seemed to be closed to me. Yet one day, I received a telephone call from my friend, George Otis, who founded High Adventure Ministries and had obtained a broadcast license in southern Lebanon. Due to the struggle in Beirut between the Lebanese, Palestinians, and Syrians, the Christian president of Lebanon, Camille Chamoun, instructed his son, Dany Chamoun, to establish a separate enclave in southern Lebanon on the border of Israel. Dany then selected an army officer, a Major Haddad, to lead this virtually autonomous region. George Otis made contact with Major Haddad and received from him a license for a radio station. Later on, George secured a license for a television station. However, such an undertaking was beyond the expertise of High Adventure Ministries. George contacted me and said, "I will not delay the coming of the Lord by trying to hold on to this license. I believe the Lord has chosen CBN to use it, and I am willing to give the license to you if you can build the station."

This seemed like an answer to prayer, but I realized it was fraught with danger. This was a war zone, and there was a very real possibility that any investment we made in a television station in southern Lebanon could be lost without recourse in the event of military action in that area. I needed to receive guidance from the Holy Spirit to know what to do.

So Dede and I prayed, and afterward I said, "What did God show you?" Her answer was, "I have a verse from Isaiah, but I don't understand what it means." I looked at it and was astounded. It was Isaiah 29:17–18: "In a very short time, will not Lebanon be turned into a fertile field and the fertile field seem like a forest? In that day the deaf will hear the words of the scroll, and out of gloom and darkness the eyes of the blind will see" (NIV). I said to Dede, "This is amazing! The station is in southern Lebanon, and the Lord is telling us that this will be a means to bring the Gospel to that whole area." I had heard from the Holy Spirit clearly that this was the way to go, but I wanted further confirmation.

The Bible tells us about a farmer visited by an angel who told him to prepare a rebellion against the Midianites. The farmer, whose name was Gideon, wanted further confirmation. He told YHWH that he would put out a sheepskin, known as a fleece, on the dry ground. If it was wet, he would take it as a sign to assemble an Israeli armed force. When he awoke, he took up the fleece. The ground around it was dry, and the fleece was soaking wet. Just to be certain, Gideon then asked for the reverse—the ground to be wet and the fleece to be dry. The next day, it came out exactly as he had requested. The Holy Spirit of God gave this man clear direction before he undertook what seemed to be an impossible armed conflict.

Consider the guidance Gideon received. He was visited by an angel. The angel demonstrated dramatic wonders before him. The fleece he put out twice came back as he requested. Armed with this direction, he put together a band of brave men who were victorious in battle.

The Holy Spirit had clearly spoken to me and Dede about the station in Lebanon. That should have been more than enough for us to act. But because of the magnitude of this decision, I went one step further. I frankly do not advise this course of action for Christians who are seeking the will of God. Nevertheless, I did so, and here is how God miraculously answered me.

I said, "Lord, if you want us to go forward with the television station in southern Lebanon, send me something of gold." I told my secretary to be on the lookout for something of gold—I was thinking about a South African or possibly a U.S. gold coin. Instead of that, the Lord absolutely amazed me.

The voluminous CBN mail was delivered to a post office address in Portsmouth, Virginia. However, I had a personal post office box in a suburb of Portsmouth called Churchland. I used that address for personal bills that did not need to be processed through the company mail system. Within a couple of days of my request to the Lord for something gold, I met Dede at a restaurant in Norfolk, and on the way to our meeting she stopped by the Churchland post office to pick up our mail. Remember, none of my friends knew of the existence of this post office box, and yet among the letters that Dede brought me that night was a letter from my friend who I mentioned earlier, Frank Foglio. He said, "I have in my possession three solid gold coins struck in a mold by Pablo Picasso." He enclosed a picture of the beautiful coin and offered to sell one to me at a reasonable price. I must say when the Holy Spirit gives guidance, he doesn't do it halfway! I was unable to purchase the coin, but Frank later gave it to us along with its certificate of authenticity signed by Pablo Picasso's daughter, Paloma. We still have it as one of our treasured possessions, showing miraculous guidance from the Holy Spirit.

I called George Otis and told him of the multiple confirmations I'd had, and that I was prepared to receive the television license for southern Lebanon and move forward. We named the station Middle East Television, and for years it broadcast in both English and Arabic throughout the entire region.

The Holy Spirit has infinite ability to answer the prayers of His servants. Throughout history we have seen men and women who have received visions, dreams, visitations by angels, and the still small voice of the Holy Spirit leading them along.

Of course, we all have available to us the word of God found in the Scriptures. Paul wrote to Timothy, "All scripture is God-breathed and is useful for teaching, rebuking, correcting and training in righteousness, so that the servant of God may be thoroughly equipped for every good work" (2 Timothy 3:16–17 NIV). Furthermore, the Bible tells us, "How can a young man cleanse his way? By taking heed according to Your word.... Your word I have hidden in my heart, that I might not sin against You" (Psalm 119:9, 11 NKJV).

I think it's fair to say that at least 90 percent of all questions dealing with personal guidance can be solved with a clear understanding of the Word of God. I am not talking about fanciful proof-texting or verses taken out of context. It is certainly unwise to attempt to be led by a verse of Scripture tortured beyond the correct meaning of a word or phrase. This I can say with certainty: if a believer sincerely cries out to the Holy Spirit for guidance and direction, the Holy Spirit will move Heaven and Earth to keep His servant from being misled.

Let me give you a couple of footnotes to the whole matter of God's guidance. The Word tells us to "not forsake wisdom" (Proverbs 4:6 NIV) and that "by the mouth of two or three witnesses every word shall be established" (2 Corinthians 13:1 NKJV). Too many cults in this world have given up on normal human wisdom to lead a group of people down an erroneous path on the strength of some supposed vision or revelation. Remember the words of the Apostle Paul, who said, "But though we, or an angel from heaven, preach any other gospel unto you than that which we have preached unto you, let him be cursed" (Galatians 1:8 KJV).

The Bible tells us that "one who walks with wise people will be wise" (Proverbs 13:20 NASB). I should make clear at this point that "the fear of the Lord is the beginning of wisdom, and knowledge of the Holy One is understanding" (Proverbs 9:10 NIV). Nevertheless, many people in secular pursuits, whether in business or government or medicine or education or sports or any other endeavor, have shown great wisdom in what they have done. There is nothing wrong in seeking to emulate the wise course of action taken by these people. What was J. C. Penney's secret of success? Why was Henry Ford successful in his manufacturing? What did Thomas Edison do to bring forth his many inventions? What secrets in financial investing are used by the man known as the "Sage of Omaha," Warren Buffett? What tactics did successful generals throughout the ages employ? What brought about their success, and what brought about their failures?

For example, Robert Kiyosaki's book *Rich Dad Poor Dad* highlights the juxtaposition between a life of wisdom and a life of folly. In this, he pointed out the steps that the rich dad took to bring prosperity to himself and his family, and then pointed out the steps that the poor dad took that led him to poverty and misery.

I am grateful personally for the three educational institutions where I studied and gained three degrees. I believe in gleaning the good and leaving behind some of the philosophical underpinnings which are contrary to the Bible.

The Book of Psalms begins with these words: "Blessed is the man who walks not in the counsel of the ungodly, nor stands in the path of sinners, nor sits in the seat of the scornful; but his delight is in the law of the Lord" (Psalm 1:1–2 NKJV). We need the counsel of godly people, and we should be humble enough to learn from them. I actually am instructed more by the mistakes that prominent people make than by the right courses of action they take.

We obviously should not follow the activity of the ungodly regardless of how prosperous they may seem to be. At the same time, the counsel of godly friends can be very helpful when we seek guidance for a particular course of action. However, I would caution against exposing the words given to us by the Holy Spirit before they come to pass. It is so easy to receive scorn and discouragement, and to be deterred from carrying out the will of God by the advice of so-called experts who do not have the mind of the Lord. I don't believe I exaggerate when I can say that for every ten people who say a goal could be achieved, there are at least ninety who can give you reasons why it will fail. Be very careful to avoid those who are known as negative thinkers. Many are ashamed that they themselves have not endeavored to accomplish anything, and they take delight in trying to frustrate the plans of those who are on course to succeed.

CHAPTER 22

WHEN THE JEWS LEFT EGYPT

When the Jews left Egypt and entered the Promised Land, they were surrounded on every side by races of people who observed customs and held beliefs directly contrary to the teachings of YHWH. They sacrificed their children to a pagan god. They freely carried on adulterous affairs and immorality. They practiced various kinds of incest. There was bestiality and homosexuality. They worshiped the sun, moon, and stars, set up asherah poles to worship the goddess Astarte, and they engaged in other practices which God had told His people would cause the land to "vomit them out." From a ban against marriage with heathens, there arose a body of teaching forbidding social interaction between Jews and Gentiles. Even after the resurrection of Jesus, His orthodox Jewish disciples, such as Peter, still refused contact with the Gentiles.

While the Apostle Peter was visiting the house of Simon the Tanner in Joppa on the Mediterranean seacoast, an angel appeared to a godly Roman centurion named Cornelius. As this Roman officer prayed, the Holy Spirit gave him a vision of an angel of God, who informed him that his prayers had been heard. The angel directed him in the vision to send servants to Joppa to bring back a man named Peter, who was staying with Simon the Tanner by the sea.

At the same time, the Holy Spirit caused Peter to fall into a trance while he waited for his midday meal; while in that trance, he saw a sheet being lowered from Heaven. In it was all manner of unclean animals. Then the voice of the Holy Spirit spoke to Peter, saying, "Get up, Peter. Kill and eat" (Acts 10:13 NIV). But Peter, the orthodox Jew, exclaimed, "Surely not, Lord! . . . I have never eaten anything impure or unclean" (Acts 10:14 NIV). The voice of the Holy Spirit replied, "Do not call anything impure that God has made clean" (Acts 10:15 NIV).

As Peter awoke, he was informed that men from Cornelius had come and asked for him. The Holy Spirit spoke to Peter and said, "Get up and go downstairs. Do not hesitate to go with them, for I have sent them" (Acts 10:20 NIV).

Despite his misgivings, Peter had clear guidance. He had a vision and a clear word from the Holy Spirit to go without doubting. So he set out on the road to the house of Cornelius. When he arrived, he found that Cornelius had gathered several friends to hear what he had to say. Peter explained to the assembled group that he was an orthodox Jew and wasn't permitted to have any social contact with them. However, he had been told by the Holy Spirit to come to deliver a message. Peter preached to them about the crucifixion of Jesus and His resurrection. As he spoke these words, the assembled Romans heard and by faith believed on Jesus as the Savior of the world.

At that moment, the Holy Spirit fell upon them, and they began to speak in tongues and glorify the Lord. We also see that

> the circumcised believers that had come with Peter were astonished that the gift of the Holy Spirit had been poured out even on Gentiles. For they heard them speaking in tongues and praising God. Then Peter said, "Surely no one can stand in the way of their being baptized with water. They have received the Holy Spirit just as we have." (Acts 10:45–47 NIV)

For the first time in the history of the Christian Church, Gentiles had believed in Jesus, been baptized by the Holy Spirit, and were accepted into the fellowship of believers. This was precisely the message that Jesus Christ had left with His people—that after the Holy Spirit had baptized them, they would be witnesses to Him "in Jerusalem, and in all Judea and Samaria, and to the ends of the earth" (Acts 1:8 NIV).

If a person stands in Joppa, he can look out onto the entire Mediterranean Sea and realize this was the place where the Holy Spirit chose to launch the Christian Church throughout the Mediterranean world and the entire Roman Empire.

However, as this was taking place, an orthodox Jewish zealot named Saul of Tarsus was intent on arresting Christians and even seeing them stoned to death. Saul and a group of what I believe were temple guards were on the way to Damascus to arrest the Christian believers. As Saul neared Damascus, a light surrounded him and he fell to the ground. A voice spoke: "'Saul, Saul, why do you persecute me?' 'Who are you, Lord?' Saul asked. 'I am Jesus, whom you are persecuting,' he replied. 'Now get up and go into the city, and you will be told what you must do'" (Acts 9:4–6 NIV).

Saul was led blind into Damascus. At the same time,

> in Damascus there was a disciple named Ananias. The Lord called to him in a vision, "Ananias!"
>
> "Yes, Lord," he answered.
>
> The Lord told him, "Go to the house of Judas on Straight Street and ask for a man from Tarsus named Saul, for he is praying. In a vision he has seen a man named Ananias come and place his hands on him to restore his sight." (Acts 9:10–12 NIV)

Of course, Ananias was like many of us who think we can remind the Lord of things that He "isn't aware of." Ananias said, "Lord…I have heard many reports about this man and all the harm he has done to your holy people in Jerusalem" (Acts 9:13 NIV). By this he implied that the Lord had the wrong guy. But the Lord corrected Ananias and said, "This man is my chosen instrument to proclaim my name to the Gentiles and their kings and to the people of Israel. I will show him how much he must suffer for my name" (Acts 9:15–16 NIV).

In obedience, Ananias went to the place where Saul was staying. He told Saul he had come to pray for his healing and that he would receive the power of the Holy Spirit. As he prayed for him, scales fell from Saul's eyes, and I presume at that moment he was baptized in the Holy Spirit. Saul the persecutor then went to Jerusalem and spoke mightily in the name of Jesus. Scripture tells us that "the church throughout Judea, Galilee and Samaria enjoyed a time of peace and was strengthened. Living in the fear of the Lord and encouraged by the Holy Spirit, it increased in numbers" (Acts 9:31 NIV).

The Holy Spirit was perfecting His Church, taking away obstacles, opening up the hearts of potential believers, and strengthening the fellowship. However, there was one thing that the Holy Spirit also accomplished dramatically. He purged deceit from the body of believers.

We are told that in the early Church there was extraordinary generosity. Believers sold their possessions and brought the money to the apostles, who were then able to buy goods and distribute them among those in the assembly. Acts 5 tells us about a man named Ananias who had a field and sold it. He hated to give away 100 percent of the proceeds, so he held part back and brought the rest to Peter. The Holy Spirit enabled Peter to sense something was wrong, so he asked Ananias if this was indeed 100 percent of the proceeds from the sale of his land. Ananias replied in the affirmative.

Peter knew he was lying, so he said, "When the money was yours, you could have kept it. But why did you lie to the Holy Spirit?" (my paraphrase). Because of that deceit, Ananias dropped dead. Shortly thereafter his wife, Sapphira, came. Peter asked if she had given 100 percent of the proceeds of the sale of the land to the Lord. She replied in the affirmative. Peter again said, "How could you conspire to test the Spirit of the Lord?

Listen! The feet of the men who buried your husband are at the door, and they will carry you out also" (Acts 5:9 NIV). And Sapphira dropped dead.

The judgment upon this young couple seems extreme. But we have found that a little evil over the years can grow into a huge evil. The Holy Spirit was not willing to allow any taint of evil to pollute the beautiful fellowship that He had established in the early Church.

Now we turn to the man who was the apostle to the Gentiles. The apostles and brothers in Judea heard that the Gentiles had received the Word of God. When Peter went to Jerusalem, he explained what happened at the house of Cornelius. Those scattered in the persecution were telling the message of the Lord in Cyprus and Cyrene and Antioch, and they also began to tell the Greeks about the good news of Jesus. A great number of people believed and turned to the Lord.

The elders of the church in Jerusalem decided to send Barnabas to encourage them, and Barnabas sought out Paul to accompany him in this task. When Barnabas found Paul, he took him to Antioch, and they stayed with the church for an entire week, teaching a great number of people the truths of Christianity. In fact, Scripture indicates that the disciples were first called Christians there.

At the church in Antioch, there were prophets and teachers from various parts of the Mediterranean world. As they were worshiping the Lord and fasting, the Holy Spirit said, "Set apart for me Barnabas and Saul for the work to which I have called them" (Acts 13:2 NIV). When they had fasted and prayed, they placed their hands on them and sent them off. The two of them, sent on the way by the Holy Spirit, went down to Seleucia and then sailed to Cyprus. Here again, we see the Holy Spirit of God calling people, directing them, and showing them the path He wants them to follow to build the Church.

CHAPTER 23

CARNAL DIVISIONS IN THE CHURCH

If we could picture ourselves in the Greek-speaking cities in Asia Minor that the Apostle Paul visited, perhaps Athens or Corinth, we would realize that the early Christians did not come from the upper strata of society or from the educated classes. They were simple laborers, shopkeepers, and small businesspeople who had only a rudimentary education. As the Apostle Paul said, "Not many mighty, not many noble, are called. But God has chosen the foolish things of the world to put to shame the wise, and God has chosen the weak things of the world to put to shame the things which are mighty" (1 Corinthians 1:26–27 NKJV).

But what happened when the power of the Holy Spirit came upon these humble people? Suddenly they received supernatural visions and dreams. They could lay hands on the sick, and they were healed. They could move in the *charismata* or revelatory gifts that gave them abilities members of their peer group couldn't imagine. It is easy to assume that some of the early Christians, filled with the power of the Holy Spirit, became proud or arrogant and could have treated the spiritual enablements like some kind of toy. The Apostle Paul wrote to them as a father to his children, telling them, "In malice be babes, but in understanding be mature" (1 Corinthians 14:20 NKJV). He told them, "When I was a child, I spoke as a child, I understood as a child, I thought as a child; but when I became a man, I put away childish things" (1 Corinthians 13:11 NKJV).

It is exciting to pray for someone and see that person healed. It is thrilling when we hear the voice of God give us a message to deliver as His special envoy. It is a natural transition to a feeling of pride when someone is used in such an unusual way. So every Christian should keep in mind that the *charismata* come from God Himself. He is the author of the miraculous, and His blessings are not given because of our ability or holiness; they are given because of His grace and wisdom.

In the early Church there was clearly pride among unlearned people, just as in the Church today. Pride and a party spirit[1] can develop among those who are not fully grounded in the faith. Scripture tells us to be eager to maintain the unity of the Spirit and the bonds of peace until we come into the knowledge of a perfect man under the fullness of Jesus Christ. Remember, God resists the proud but gives grace to the humble (1 Peter 5:5). There is nothing that any of us have, whether education or

---

[1] This by no means describes a political affiliation or preference, but rather refers to an allegiance to a particular form of doctrine or being a follower of a particular religious leader.

wisdom or wealth, that did not come from a loving Father. We should constantly be on the alert against pride and a party spirit.

Paul was a Hebrew, a Roman citizen who thought and wrote in the Greek language. Greek is very precise concerning the emotion we know as love. From *eros* we get the word "erotic," and that is sexual love between a man and a woman. *Phileo* is a type of brotherly love used in naming Philadelphia, the "City of Brotherly Love." Then there is *agape*, the sacrificial love that Jesus Christ showed to His disciples and ultimately the whole world when He died for us on the cross at Calvary.

The Apostle Paul realized the importance of bringing clarity to these young Christians over whom the Holy Spirit had given him apostleship and spiritual fatherhood. He wanted them to clearly understand that the Church to which they belonged had been established by the Holy Spirit on the foundation of Jesus Christ. He warned them about carnal divisions and the type of factionalism that resulted from pitting one Christian leader against another. He told them his message was not based on appealing words of Greek wisdom. Instead, it was accompanied by a demonstration of the power of the Holy Spirit so their faith would rest not on men's intelligence, but on the power of God. He then quoted from Isaiah, "Eye has not seen, nor ear heard, nor have entered into the heart of man the things which God has prepared for those who love Him" (1 Corinthians 2:9 NKJV). But he declared the Holy Spirit had revealed them. "For the Spirit searches all things, yes, the deep things of God" (1 Corinthians 2:10 NKJV).

The Apostle Paul then went on to explain in detail the further working of the Holy Spirit. He said, "In the same way no one knows the thoughts of God except the Spirit of God. What we have received is not the spirit of the world, but the Spirit who is from God, so that we may understand what God has freely given us" (1 Corinthians 2:11–12 NIV). In the Greek language, the word for soul is *psuche*. The word for body is *soma*. The word for Spirit is *pneuma*. Some people have a psychosomatic illness, which is an illness from the soul that affects the body. From the word *psuche* we get the term *psychic*. We're certainly forbidden to stir up our psychic powers. I don't question the fact that there are indeed people who can demonstrate extraordinary feats of knowledge about what they claim are psychic revelations. But these revelations do not come from God and very often can be manipulated by spirits from the enemy.

When Paul wrote to the church in Corinth, he told them clearly that the soulish man (*psucheikos*) "receiveth not the things of the Spirit of God: for they are foolishness unto him" (1 Corinthians 2:14 KJV). But the man motivated by the Spirit of God "judges all things, yet he himself is rightly judged by no one" (1 Corinthians 2:15 NKJV).

When Jesus Christ was on Earth, He informed His disciples that no man could come to Him unless he was led by God. The Apostle Paul amplified that very clearly when he said, "No one can say that Jesus is Lord except by the Holy Spirit" (1 Corinthians 12:3 NKJV). In other words, the statement which affirms a person's experience as a Christian is directly given by the Holy Spirit. It is certainly not a psychic experience. It is a spiritual experience. And again, we emphasize the words of Paul, who said, "For 'who has known the mind of the LORD [YHWH] that he may instruct Him?' But we have the mind of Christ" (1 Corinthians 2:16 NKJV).

CHAPTER 24

MIRACLES IN MY LIFE

Around the year 1900, a young man endowed by the Holy Spirit with a remarkable prophetic understanding traveled from Russia to the Armenian section of Turkey. He explained to the Armenian people that God had given him a revelation—a great persecution of the Christian people in Turkey was coming, and they should sell what they had, take the money, and travel to America. He actually drew a map showing the route from Turkey to New York and from New York to the Los Angeles area of California. As you can imagine, most of the people who heard his message didn't believe it and refused to give up the comfortable life they had been enjoying for many decades.

Tragically, the vision of the young Russian came to pass in what is called the Armenian Genocide. After World War I, the Ottoman Empire was breaking out, and a new Turkey came into being. The leaders were called the "Young Turks," and Kemal Atatürk was their leader. Although Atatürk pledged to make

Turkey a secular state, he only did so after proclaiming that all non-Muslims should be removed from the country. At this point, the Armenian Genocide began, lasting from 1915 to 1917, in which horrible atrocities were committed against adults and children alike. Words are inadequate to explain the horrors visited upon these innocent people. Nevertheless, it happened, and those Christian Armenians who did not heed the voice of the prophet sent to them lived to suffer the agony of their decision. But for those who did, a bright future lay ahead.

At least one family, the Shakarians, believed the young man. They sold their possessions, took the money, and took transportation through Europe, across the Atlantic, then across the United States to California. When they arrived in Los Angeles, the Azusa Street Revival was taking place. These Armenian Christians felt completely at home with this type of worship that they had known in their home country.

Isaac Shakarian began selling produce from a pushcart. From those proceeds, he bought a herd of cattle and went into the dairy business. Before he died many years later, Isaac Shakarian had acquired large land holdings in Southern California and was running the largest independent dairy in the country. His son, Demos, who was brought up in that environment, became in his own right an extraordinarily successful businessman and landowner.

One night when young Demos was in prayer, the wall in his room appeared like fire, and he saw men by the thousands all over the world raising their hands and praising God. On the strength of that vision, he called together a few of his friends to meet for a breakfast prayer meeting at Clifton's Cafeteria in Los

Angeles. Out of this initial prayer meeting came an organization known as the Full Gospel Businessmen's Fellowship (FGBF)—an organization of Spirit-filled men whose earnest desire was to see the message of the full Gospel spread throughout America and around the world.

One by one, Spirit-filled businessmen were chosen as chapter heads of the FGBF in their respective cities. After several years, these men elected a group of international directors, who were given charge of the organization. They, in turn, attracted their friends and businessmen in cities all across the nation to their chapter meetings. As the organization grew, the meetings expanded to larger-scale regional gatherings which took place over a period of several days. In each of these gatherings, well-known Christian leaders were invited to speak, and the meetings of the FGBF were highlights for those who attended.

At a regional FGBF convention in Washington, D.C., in the 1960s, the featured speaker was famed evangelist Kathryn Kuhlman. She was scheduled to conduct what was called a "miracle service." Unfortunately, at the last minute, Kathryn was unable to attend, and a vacancy opened. The regional directors looked around for a speaker and settled on me as a candidate. They asked me to go to Washington on a Saturday afternoon to conduct a "miracle service" for a crowd of several thousand people who would meet in a large hotel ballroom.

When a person is asked to teach, typically the only expectation is an exposition of the Bible. If he's asked to preach or lead an evangelistic meeting, he only has to invite people to give their hearts in faith to Jesus Christ. If, on the other hand, he is asked to perform miracles, then there's no way out—there must be miracles!

On that Saturday afternoon, I stood with some fear and trepidation before that large audience to ask for miracles. The Lord led me to speak about the Syrian general Naaman. He was so filled with pride that his leprosy couldn't be healed until he obediently dipped in the waters of the Jordan River.

After I spoke, I asked the audience to join me in praising God, and this we did with great enthusiasm. We lifted our hands, we praised God, we cried out for His blessing—and suddenly the miracles began. The Holy Spirit began to flow through me in words of knowledge, and I called out healings all over the room. People stood and testified that miracles had taken place. It was a demonstration of the power of God such as I had seldom seen.

In one instance, the Lord told me that someone was praying for $7,200 and that He was going to answer this prayer. Remarkably, a couple of the attendees had left the meeting and were driving away, listening to the radio. They had been praying for exactly $7,200, and this was an answer to their prayer.

But more particularly, the Lord gave me a word of knowledge that God was healing someone with a deteriorating spine. To my right, not far from the platform, an Air Force lieutenant general was facing forced retirement because of a deteriorating spine. Like General Naaman, this officer was too proud to acknowledge his dependence on God. But at that moment, because of the word of knowledge, he opened his heart to the power of the Holy Spirit, and his spine was miraculously healed.

I will never forget that day, as wave after wave of the power of God went through that audience and the Holy Spirit, through the manifestation of words of knowledge, brought forth miracles and rejoicing to all assembled.

Although this one glorious time stands out in my memory, my cohost on *The 700 Club* and I also witness miraculous demonstrations of God's power every time we pray together on the air.

When I first began broadcasting, I led the audience in prayer, but there was never a word of knowledge. One day I was the sole host on the program, and I was sitting at the desk in front of the microphone, asking people to begin to pray. As we prayed, something strange came over me. I smelled peanut butter. I could taste peanut butter, and I even felt surrounded by peanut butter. So I said, "I'm not sure what this is, but somebody in this audience who is involved with peanut butter has a heart condition."

It turned out that one of our audience members indeed was involved with peanut butter. She had dropped a jar of it in her kitchen, and she was on her hands and knees wiping it up at that moment with the television playing in the background. As the word of knowledge went forth, she knew she was the recipient and claimed the healing of her heart condition in the midst of the peanut butter. I know it's somewhat amusing, but that was my introduction on the air to moving into words of knowledge.

Since that time, I have seen God do absolutely remarkable things. Let me give you one example.

As I was praying, the Lord showed me a woman with a broken foot in a cast, watching the program, and that He was healing her by His power. My program that day, as I recall, took place on a Monday. Two days later, a woman in Beverly Hills broke her ankle and was put in a cast. (Remember, she had not broken her ankle when the word of knowledge went forth. But God does not live in time. He lives in eternity. And with Him there is no beginning or end...it's all eternal.) That taped program played on the air in Beverly Hills the following Monday when indeed there was a woman with an ankle in a cast watching; she was touched and healed by the word that had been given to describe her condition before she even had it.

I recall another interesting report which came to us from Africa. It seems that a woman in Nigeria was watching a tape of *The 700 Club* on her sickbed. While she was in a relatively helpless state, a gang of young thugs broke into her house and advanced menacingly toward her. As they moved forward, our taped program was playing on a television in the background. Suddenly the young thugs jumped in fright and fled the house because they sensed the presence of a spiritual being coming out of the television broadcast. I am unable to say how God attaches Himself to a taped broadcast that manifests so much power it frightens burglars, but nevertheless this is what happened.

It is simply astounding that the Holy Spirit of God will give to His people revelation and power to heal members of an audience throughout the nation and around the world.

I remember one instance that is somewhat amusing. As I was praying, I felt the Holy Spirit saying He was healing somebody's knee. I said that somebody's knee was being healed and added, "I believe that it's the right knee." Now that broadcast was taped, and the tape was sent to a distant city to be played a week later. A woman in that city was watching the program, and as I said, "The right knee is being healed," she said to the television, "No dummy, it's the left knee!" And then on the tape, my voice said, "No, it's not the right knee, it's the left knee," and the woman's left knee was healed. How can a viewer talk to a tape of a week-old live broadcast and have it actually respond to her statement?

As I have walked with the Spirit of God, I have realized His incredible wisdom. As we now have recorded, thousands and thousands of suffering individuals have been identified—often by name—and healed by a word of knowledge given through me or a cohost.

Before I give you more specifics, let me explain what I'm talking about. Both the word of wisdom and the word of knowledge are received by the individual's inner man, either by what would be called an impression or an actual voice. I am absolutely not talking about some type of psychic manifestation, but a clear word from the Holy Spirit of God.

I feel that the Spirit of God works in praise. Scripture tells us, "Enter into his gates with thanksgiving, and into his courts with praise" (Psalm 100:4 KJV). As we praise God, His Spirit begins to speak back to us. Always the manifestation of the Holy Spirit is given to strengthen and edify the body of Christ. These are not toys with which to be played, but grace gifts to those who are humbly open to God's working.

Here now are several instances taken from *The 700 Club* daily program which I have been privileged to host for over five decades.

Rebecca of Knoxville, Tennessee

After Rebecca had open-heart surgery on February 3, 2008, her vocal chords were significantly damaged. This devastated Rebecca because she could no longer sing.

While watching *The 700 Club* on March 18, 2020, she heard me say through a word of knowledge, "Someone is a singer and you have a problem with your voice box. Put your hand on your throat right now and believe God." Rebecca instantly knew this was for her, so she shot off her couch and claimed it. She was immediately able to sing and chose as her first song "Amazing Grace."

Nila of Aztec, New Mexico

Nila felt terrible for her friend Larry, who suffered from a significant bowel issue. It was so severe that he had to go to the ER four times with excruciating pain. His doctor diagnosed it as a blockage and suggested surgery. Nila had another friend who also knew about Larry's condition. This friend watched *The 700 Club* on March 4, 2020, and heard me pray, "Someone is dealing with an issue in their intestines. A blockage is being removed; you will feel much better."

This friend sent Nila a video copy of that segment. They both claimed it for Larry. During his next appointment, Larry's doctor confirmed the blockage was gone!

Wendy of Fallbrook, California

Just before Christmas 2019, the unthinkable happened to Wendy of Fallbrook, California. A man driving a Ford F-150 hit her with his truck while she was standing in front of Home Depot. The CT scan showed severe brain trauma and a concussion. Since then, Wendy had suffered with chronic dizziness.

She watched *The 700 Club* on March 26, 2020, and heard me pray, "Someone with a problem in your brain. There's some fluid or something in the brain tissues…touch your hand over your forehead and be healed in Jesus's name." Through this word of knowledge, Wendy immediately realized her dizziness was gone. She even shook her head around and did all sorts of things she hadn't done for three months!

Louis of Whiting, New Jersey

In September 2019, Louis of Whiting, New Jersey, had a routine knee surgery and started physical therapy. Regrettably, during his first session, he was told to do an exercise and immediately heard a loud "pop!" He now had a torn quadriceps in addition to his knee issue.

Louis watched *The 700 Club* on March 19, 2020, and heard me pray, "Someone has ripped the right quadriceps muscle (maybe while exercising), torn it, and it has been very painful. Right now, the pain is leaving." Louis knew this word was for him, and God instantly healed him! He hasn't had any pain since.

Mary Lou of Cibolo, Texas

Over time, Mary Lou's shoulder started showing wear and tear from literally carrying gallons of water up three flights of stairs. Her shoulder bone started to protrude, pointing upward. It was extremely painful.

While watching *The 700 Club* on March 25, 2020, Mary Lou heard me pray, "Your arm—it's very painful. Right now, you will feel a warmth in that break. Those bones are knitting together miraculously; your arm is completely well." She believed and could tell instantly that her shoulder was completely healed!

During the same show, I also prayed for someone's throat, saying, "Touch your throat right now, and you are healed." Mary Lou experienced unusual phlegm as a result of a surgery she'd had twenty years ago. God healed both conditions immediately through these words of knowledge!

Barbara of Lima, Ohio

Whenever Barbara went to the store, she hoped a scooter would be available. She had a bad hip and couldn't put pressure on it.

While watching *The 700 Club* on March 18, 2020, Barbara heard me pray, "Someone who has a hip injury…arthritis or dislocation will be healed. You might feel something pop into place." By faith she believed for healing to manifest. Since this word of knowledge, Barbara has been able to walk up and down the stairs and through the store without a scooter!

Adrienne of Phoenix, Arizona

When Adrienne discovered an abnormality in her breast several months ago, she hoped and prayed for the best. Her doctor told her to come back for more tests.

Meanwhile, Adrienne watched *The 700 Club*. On January 7, 2020, she heard me pray, "Someone has a lump in your breast—touch your breast, and in the name of Jesus the lump is disappearing as we speak." Adrienne claimed this word. When she returned to her doctor, the imaging proved that the lump was gone!

Mary of Fort Worth, Texas

While working her normal schedule at a nursing home, Mary developed a cough. Naturally, she feared the worst and thought it could be COVID-19. Mary watched *The 700 Club* on March 17, 2020, and heard me say her name. I prayed, "Someone, you've had a condition which is congestion in your lungs and it's not coronavirus—I believe the name is Mary. I want you to cough now and blow out all the air in your lungs and then breathe deeply, and your lungs will be completely healed."

By faith, Mary followed the instructions given through this word of knowledge. She felt a burden release from her chest, stopped coughing, and hasn't coughed since! Not only did God remove Mary's affliction, but she got something else as well: she no longer fears COVID-19 and has the peace of the Holy Spirit.

Rhunette of Duluth, Minnesota

Since December 2019, Rhunette had suffered from two serious health issues. She watched *The 700 Club* on March 4, 2020, and heard a word of knowledge prayed for both issues! First, I prayed,

"Someone dealing with an issue in their intestines—a blockage is being removed; you will feel much better."

Then my cohost Wendy Griffith prayed, "There is a problem with your hips. Your hips and spine are out of line, and you have pain coming up the small of your back.... Your spine will be healed, and the hips aligned properly." Rhunette believed this word and was instantly healed of both conditions. She called our prayer line on March 16 still rejoicing!

Lona of King, North Carolina

After almost an entire year of distressing knee pain, things changed for Lona on April 3, 2020. That was the day she watched *The 700 Club* and heard my son, Gordon, pray, "Someone with bone-on-bone pain in the left knee doesn't want to go to the doctor. Jesus has come to you and healed that joint. You will move normally without pain." Lona believed the word, was healed, and can now move her knee freely and without pain!

Mary of Kansas City, Missouri

Mary's right shoulder had been hurting for an entire year, with no relief in sight. On April 3, 2020, she watched *The 700 Club* and heard Gordon say her name during prayer. His word of knowledge was, "Mary, you are laying your left hand on your right shoulder. You couldn't move that right shoulder and God has healed you, and you can move normally." By faith, Mary rubbed her right shoulder and was completely healed!

Deloris of Humble, Texas

Falling at any age is potentially serious, but especially for Deloris, who in March 2020 was eighty-five years old. She fell the last week of that month and injured her right side, especially in her lung area. A week later, she was watching watch *The 700 Club* when she heard Gordon pray for someone who was experiencing pain on the right side. He said, "God has healed you, and you can move normally." As Gordon prayed, Deloris put her hands on her right side and the pain disappeared. She called our prayer line in response to this word, giving God the glory for removing the pain in that area!

Jewel of Atlanta, Georgia

Jewel was eighty-three. In 2016, she was diagnosed with congestive heart failure. On August 30, 2019, Jewel watched *The 700 Club* and heard Gordon give this word of knowledge: "There's someone else; you have been diagnosed with congestive heart failure. There's pressure on your heart. You are having pain, difficulty breathing, and you have no energy. Be healed. All fluid leave now in Jesus's name. Let there be a fresh breath right now. Let there be new energy, new vitality. In Jesus's name, be healed."

My cohost Terry Meeuwsen immediately followed with, "There are many people having trouble with respiratory and all kinds of breathing issues. God is breathing new life into you right now. Inhale and receive it and exhale the old." Jewel received her healing by faith. One of her doctors confirmed she was healed (though her other doctor remained skeptical). Jewel knows her Great Physician got it right!

Nancy of Longboat Key, Florida

For seven years, Nancy suffered with rheumatoid arthritis, which began intensifying in 2018 to the point of disfiguring her hands. As she watched *The 700 Club* on March 13, 2020, Nancy heard Gordon pray over an underlying condition that caused constant pain. He said, "Be released from that pain, and may you have it no longer." Nancy felt something she likened to a "lightning bolt" go through her body. It was so strong that she had to lie down for an hour. When she went to her doctor, he confirmed that she no longer had rheumatoid arthritis! Nancy received her word of knowledge.

Martha of Kihei, Hawaii

Martha couldn't figure out what was causing (or how to fix) her lingering hoarseness. For a year, it would come and go. However, for six months, she was hoarse every single day.

While watching *The 700 Club* on March 17, 2020, Martha heard Terry Meeuwsen pray, "Someone has a raspiness in your voice that isn't normal for you, but it's been there for a while. Today is your day in Jesus and your voice will return to normal." After praying and believing this word, Martha's voice is completely normal!

Geneva of Amite City, Louisiana

A serious blockage caused Geneva's doctors to do a bowel resection, removing over two feet of her intestines. Although better, she still had chronic diarrhea.

While watching *The 700 Club* on March 10, 2020, Geneva heard Terry Meeuwsen pray, "Someone has issues with your stomach, digesting your food. Some of you have ulcers in the lining of your stomach and many issues with the stomach. You are being healed right now." Geneva placed her hand on her stomach by faith and, sure enough, received complete healing through this word!

Joseph of Shrewsbury, Massachusetts

In 2014, Joseph received the disappointing diagnosis of spinal stenosis in both hips. His pain was unbearable and made it extremely difficult to keep his part-time job, which required standing all day. Walking became so difficult that he eventually had to quit. On October 13, 2019, he found himself in the worst, most excruciating pain he had ever felt. He went to the hospital.

Joseph watched *The 700 Club* and heard Terry Meeuwsen speak healing through a word of knowledge for someone with spinal stenosis. He has been healed ever since and can walk seven miles without any pain!

Sue of Ironwood, Michigan

Sue's frustrating chronic cough started when she was fifty-five years old. She is now sixty-four. During the March 24, 2020, broadcast of *The 700 Club*, Sue heard Terry Meeuwsen pray for someone who had "difficulty swallowing with a very bad cough; it's not the coronavirus but a chronic condition. You are being healed of everything that causes that cough."

Sue believed this word and, after eight and a half years, is completely healed!

Carol of Virginia Beach, Virginia

Carol's life drastically changed in 2014 when she fell and sustained many serious injuries. She had six crushed vertebrae, a head injury, chronic migraines, and a torn rotator cuff. She could not stand for more than ten minutes at a time.

On March 4, 2020, while watching *The 700 Club*, Carol heard my cohost Wendy Griffith pray, "There is a problem with your hips. Your hips and spine are out of line, and you have pain coming up the small of your back. It is not scoliosis, but it feels that way. Your spine will be healed, and the hips aligned properly." Carol claimed this word, can now stand for long periods of time, and her sleep has been restored. She was scheduled for another surgery but, at this rate, doesn't think it will be necessary!

CHAPTER 25

THE SPIRIT LEADS ME IN CHINA

As I have grown in the Christian life, it has been my delight to realize that the Holy Spirit can speak to me not only during earnest times of prayer, but also in my day-to-day walk. In difficult situations, He can give me an appropriate word that is perfectly suitable. Let me explain how the power of the Holy Spirit was active in my life while I was visiting China and was forced to speak to the Chinese people through an interpreter.

I have made several visits to China. On the first, shortly after the Cultural Revolution in the late 1970s, I was escorted by a government-approved tour guide. The Chinese men were desperately poor and wore drab-looking uniforms similar to those worn by their former leader, Mao Tse-tung. As I recall, there were only two colors—blue and gray. Beyond that, there was no special adornment. When I first visited China, there were hardly any cars. Most of the people either walked or rode bicycles.

One evening, I went outside to see if I could speak to some of the people on the street. In those days, the Chinese people were very friendly, but they were enormously curious about any Westerner like me and would gather around just to see a simple camera. I left my hotel room and went out with an interpreter into the darkened streets of the village. As I was surrounded by a very friendly group of people, I asked the Lord how to speak to them.

The Holy Spirit gave me a message: I said I had come to tell them about a God who wanted to prosper and bless them. As I spoke under the power of the Holy Spirit, it was like a scene out of the New Testament. These wonderful people actually laughed in joy at the fact that I was going to tell them how the Creator God would prosper and bless them. I invited them to pray with me, and all but one in the crowd surrounding me obediently bowed their heads and prayed to receive Jesus Christ as their Savior. I knew without question that the Holy Spirit would indeed touch China and many other nations around the world. I saw demonstrated the incredible power that was given to me as His servant to speak the words of Jesus Christ under the anointing of the Holy Spirit.

A few years later, I ran for the Republican nomination for the presidency of the United States and founded the Christian Coalition, which was playing a major role in grassroots politics at the time. When George W. Bush was elected president in 2000, the Chinese leadership accorded me special privileges. I told the committee selected to welcome dignitaries that I wanted to meet with Prime Minister Zhu Rongji. Before long, arrangements were made for such a meeting.

I traveled to the compound where the prime minister lived, was ushered into a large reception hall, and seated on a slightly raised dais across from him. Behind me sat a Chinese lady who would translate his words to me; behind him sat another lady who could interpret my English into Chinese for him. Sitting on the floor in front of us in two parallel rows were the members of my traveling party. I wanted to explain to the prime minister that Christians were not a threat, but were good citizens and would be the source of prosperity in his nation. As we talked, I was not merely listening to the voice of the interpreter, but also to the voice of the Holy Spirit.

I waited patiently for the Lord to give me the necessary words in answer to his comments to me. It was a wonderful experience, because the Spirit of God knew exactly what would touch this man's heart. What the Lord shared with me to tell him was carried across China on the Xinhua News Agency. And Prime Minister Zhu Rongji actually reported our conversation to the Chinese Politburo. From that moment on, I was designated a "friend of China." On later visits, I was identified as an "old friend of China" and had access to virtually the entire country.

On one particular occasion, I was interested in helping the poor in China through our Operation Blessing. I was given an audience with the minister of poverty alleviation—the official title of a government administrator. As I spoke with him, I waited on the Holy Spirit for every single word I uttered. The Lord enabled me to press him on the definition of poverty in China. The Holy Spirit was very persistent, and before I was finished, I had learned that the definition of poverty included those who could not afford food in excess of two thousand calories a day. Then, under the inspiration of the Holy Spirit, I explained to him that our organization wanted to help him alleviate poverty among his people. Before the meeting was over, he had agreed to designate twenty-five thousand cities that we could work in to help lift the people out of poverty. In that interchange with this fine man, I waited on the Holy Spirit; He did not fail me.

CHAPTER 26

A Most Unusual Question

I'd like to relate something that happened a few years back when I led a group of Christian tourists on a visit to Israel. We toured the holy sites throughout the nation and had wonderful experiences before returning to our hotel in Jerusalem. On the evening before our departure, I was enjoying a light supper in the hotel coffee shop. Three of the ladies from the tour came to my table and said, "Brother Robertson, there's a lady in our group who is demon-possessed. Would you get a couple of the men and go cast the demons out of her?"

I know it seems selfish, but I didn't feel like leaving my dinner to go cast demons out of anybody. I finished my dinner first, and then my wife and I went to find out what the problem was. Apparently, this woman from the West Coast had suffered panic attacks and had begun screaming at night that she was dying. Her companions were alarmed. They realized that their roommate was perfectly healthy, and they couldn't account for the fact that she was having these extraordinary attacks. They jumped to the conclusion that they had to be caused by malevolent spirits, which in turn called for spiritual deliverance. I learned that they had taken the offending woman to stay in another hotel because her nightly outcries were disturbing their entire group.

Dede and I took a cab to the hotel where the woman in question was residing. We went up to her room and knocked on her door. When she opened it, she had a look of fright and desperation on her face. I explained who I was—that I was the leader of the tour group and had come with my wife to see if we could help her. She invited us into her room, and as I recall, I sat on the bed while she and my wife occupied the two available chairs. I said, "Could you tell me what's been the matter?"

She replied, "I have panic attacks, I can't breathe, and I feel I'm dying." I replied, "Have you seen a psychiatrist or a medical doctor to help you with this condition?" She replied, "Yes, I have seen a psychiatrist." I then asked, "What did the psychiatrist tell you?" She answered, "He said that I was having these attacks because I had been praying with nuns."

I replied in amazement, "A medical professional told you that?" And she said, "Yes." I knew very well that praying with nuns did not cause anybody to have panic attacks. There had to be something more. I said, "Can we pray together?" She agreed.

As I prayed, I inquired, "Lord, what is wrong with this woman?" He replied, "Ask her about her sex life."

Well, there was no way under Heaven I would ask a strange woman about the intimate details of her life, but the Lord had instructed me, so I said, "Tell me about your marriage." She said,

"I have a wonderful marriage, and I love my husband." I repeated, "You have a wonderful marriage, and you love your husband?" And she replied that this was correct.

I asked the Lord again, and He repeated, "Ask her about her sex life." I told her, "You'll have to excuse me, but I have one more question. You said you have a wonderful marriage, but can you tell me about your sex life?" She said, "I don't have any sex life."

I said, "You said you have a wonderful marriage and you love your husband, but you don't have any sex life?" "That's correct," she said.

I asked, "When did these panic attacks start?" She replied, "About the time that my husband was unable to engage in marital relations."

"And you blame yourself for that?"

"Yes."

"Do you think it was your fault?"

"Yes."

To confirm, I asked, "You started having panic attacks right after that?" "Yes," she said.

Now I realized that praying with nuns did not give anybody a panic attack, but lack of any marital relations could cause a problem if this lady felt as guilty as she did. I said, "Do you realize that what's wrong with your husband has nothing to do with you?" She answered, "I thought it was my fault."

"Your husband has a problem. Perhaps his job is too stressful to have a healthy married life. Perhaps he should see a urologist or get some kind of counseling." She asked, "Do you really think so?"

"Yes, it's not your fault."

A sense of relief began to wash over this woman's face. I said, "May I pray for you?" She agreed, and I prayed in the name of Jesus, speaking healing over that poor woman. At that moment she was freed from her guilt and her panic attacks, and she was totally set free from her problem.

A smile came over her face and she was filled with the joy of the Lord. It was the kind of transformation that any counselor would be overjoyed to see in a patient. And all this in a matter of a few minutes, because the Holy Spirit knew precisely what was in that dear woman's heart and shared the answer with me.

I cannot imagine what would have happened to that woman if three burly men had come into her room and cast a supposed demon out of her. She would have been ruined for life. But through the power of the Holy Spirit, she was set free.

I know there are psychiatrists and psychologists who believe that religious faith is some kind of psychosis, but I firmly believe that if doctors, nurses, and psychological counselors were filled with the power of God and had the anointing of the Holy Spirit, their work would be so much more effective. Think what would happen if instead of hours and hours of counseling, these men and women of science could zero in on the real problems confronting their patients and deal with them spiritually as I had with that woman in Jerusalem. Think what a transformation would take place in those patients who are stressed because of emotional trauma and not true physical or chemical imbalances.

Without question, demons are real. When Jesus Christ walked on the earth and dealt with people, no sick person ever went away without being healed. Jesus, however, knew the difference between epilepsy and paralysis, and between guilt over sin and demonic possession. He was always tender and compassionate, but because of the power of the Holy Spirit, He always knew the root cause of each problem. The remarkable thing is that this power is still given to the Church today; we need merely to be willing to exercise it.

CHAPTER 27

MANIFESTATIONS OF THE OUTPOURED SPIRIT

I n writing to the early Christians, the Apostle Paul not only delineated for them the various *charismata* or "gifts of the Spirit," but he also took time to ensure that the manifestations of the outpoured Spirit were matched by the fruit of the Spirit. He made sure they understood that if a Christian believer could perform miraculous feats like moving mountains, or if he had such great generosity that he gave all his goods to feed the poor, or if he had wisdom to understand all mysteries but lacked love, his spiritual accomplishments would have no lasting meaning.

Some of the statements that the Apostle Paul made to the church in Corinth have, in my opinion, been either misunderstood or misused. For example, Paul said, "If there are tongues, they will cease" (1 Corinthians 13:8 NASB). That statement was seized upon as a proof text for those who affirm that the miraculous gifts of the Holy Spirit, especially the Pentecostal expression of it, ceased with the early apostles.

However, the Apostle Paul meant no such thing, for he also said, "Where there is knowledge, it will pass away" (1 Corinthians 13:8 NIV). those who think that tongues are at an end would have to concede that knowledge must also be at an end. And this, of course, is absurd. Paul intended no such thing.

Paul also wrote, "For we know in part and we prophesy in part; but when the perfect comes, the partial will be done away with" (1 Corinthians 13:9–10 NASB). There are denominations that proclaim that "perfect" means the Bible; therefore, the Holy Spirit stopped working in an apostolic sense during the first one hundred years of the Church after the canon of the Bible was complete. Of course, that statement runs contrary to what Paul himself said: "For we know in part and we prophesy in part" (1 Corinthians 13:9 NASB). The Apostle Paul, who wrote a good part of the books making up the New Testament, did not claim to know everything.

I firmly believe that the power of God did not stop with the completion of the canon of Scripture. Although the Scriptures are our guide, the only perfection is Jesus Himself, and some of the manifestations of the Holy Spirit are active today and will continue to be active until He returns. As it is, we honor the Word of God, and we seek diligently to discover the words given by the Holy Spirit to anointed men of God through the ages.

Again, I say, the only thing that is perfect is Jesus Himself, and when He returns the manifestations of the Holy Spirit will not be necessary, because we will be like Him and we will see Him as He is. For now, my message is this: let us diligently seek more of the power of God's Holy Spirit that is so freely available to those who truly seek Him.

CHAPTER 28

THE SPIRIT AND THE BRIDE OF CHRIST

A closing thought... Writing in the Book of Revelation, the Apostle John saw the Holy City, the New Jerusalem, coming down from Heaven as a bride adorned for her husband. And in Revelation 22:17 we have these words: "The Spirit and the bride say, 'Come!' And let the one who hears say, 'Come!' Let the one who is thirsty come; and let the one who wishes take the free gift of the water of life" (NIV).

In Revelation, the Holy Spirit is linked with the Bride of Christ. It has been my contention in this book that the Holy Spirit is the being in the Trinity of God who deals with the Church, with humanity, with His chosen people, and with this planet that we call Earth. Now Revelation portrays the Bride of Christ as coming from Heaven, and the Spirit of God is one with the Bride, as if in some type of wedding procession. The Bible could say the Son of God and the Bride of Christ, but it says the Holy Spirit and the Bride are entering the new creation together. So here in the last book of the Bible we see the Holy Spirit once more shown as the being in the Trinity who brings to His creation—especially to His cherished—life and blessing and hope.

ADDENDUM

Our staff members have received many questions about the Holy Spirit. I will attempt to answer a few of them, which I hope will amplify what has been written in this book.

Q: Do I have to be a mature Christian to receive the Holy Spirit?

A: No, you do not. The Holy Spirit descended on those gathered at the house of Cornelius, a Roman soldier, who was not a professing Christian at all. And yet when he heard the message of salvation, he received Jesus and at that moment was baptized in the Holy Spirit. Jesus told us we're supposed to have the faith of a little child. So often it is the "mature Christians" who think they've tried everything and refuse to acknowledge that they perhaps have been going in the wrong direction.

Q: How did the Holy Spirit operate in the Old Testament? Was He present at creation? Was King David filled with the Holy Spirit?

A: A large portion of this book is devoted to the work of the Holy Spirit in the Old Testament. David wrote a psalm which said, "Take not thy holy spirit from me. Restore unto me the joy of thy salvation" (Psalm 51:11–12 KJV). As I pointed out in this book, in the Old Testament the Holy Spirit was given by God to selected prophets, holy men, and leaders. Later, on the Day of Pentecost, the Holy Spirit was poured out upon all flesh, and those who believed in Jesus Christ were filled with the Spirit.

Q: Please help me understand this verse from Romans 8:26: "In the same way, the Spirit helps us in our weakness. We do not know what we ought to pray for, but the Spirit himself intercedes for us through wordless groans" (NIV).

A: The Bible teaches us that the Holy Spirit is in touch with our spirit and that agreement with His Spirit brings about miraculous deeds. Many times as human beings, we are not aware of the situation that is confronting us, but the Holy Spirit is. He joins with our spirit and leads us in intercessory prayer that transcends what our minds are able to comprehend. We're told to "wrestle in prayer" and that the Church prayed "stretched-outedly" for Peter to be released from prison (Acts 12:5). Jesus Himself was in such agony in the Garden of Gethsemane that He actually sweat blood. It's said that John Knox of Scotland prayed in agony, "Oh God, give me Scotland or I perish." Very few know this kind of intercession, but the Holy Spirit will bring about groanings which cannot be uttered in the lives of those who are spiritually attuned.

Q: Can we accept salvation through Jesus or believe in His Lordship apart from the work of the Holy Spirit?

A: The Bible is very clear in this regard. "No one can say, 'Jesus is Lord,' except by the Holy Spirit" (1 Corinthians 12:3 NIV). The confession that brings about salvation is "Jesus is Lord." "If you confess with your mouth the Lord Jesus and believe in your heart that God has raised Him from the dead, you will be saved" (Romans 10:9 NKJV). Therefore, in answer to your question, I say emphatically, there is no salvation except what is brought about through belief in the Lord Jesus Christ which, in turn, is accomplished by the work of the Holy Spirit. All human beings are made in the image of God, and all have been given a spirit which can respond to the Spirit of God. Nevertheless, I do not believe our spirits can fully recognize the death, resurrection, and lordship of Jesus Christ without the work of the Holy Spirit.

Q: What does it mean to dance in the Spirit?

A: We're told that when the Ark of the Covenant was being brought up to Jerusalem, "David was dancing before the LORD [YHWH]" (2 Samuel 6:14 NIV). He was twirling and leaping and jumping for joy. I believe there can be spontaneous expressions of joy at the presence of God's Spirit, and humans can react like the lame man who was healed at the Gate Beautiful, when he began leaping and dancing and praising God.

Q: The Hebrew for "wind" is ruach. *Would you explain how this helps to understand the Person and the work of the Holy Spirit?*

A: On the Day of Pentecost, when the disciples were gathered in the upper room of a house, the power of God descended on them. How did He do it? There was the sound of a rushing mighty wind, which filled the place where they were sitting. Then, tongues of fire appeared upon the heads of all believers (Acts 2:1–3). The wind or breath is the symbol of the Spirit. Fire is the symbol of holiness. On the Day of Pentecost, the Spirit of God manifested as a mighty rushing wind that filled the house, and the tongues of fire represented holiness. In that one instance, there was a clear demonstration of the Holy Spirit.

Q: I haven't received the gift of tongues, and as a result some church members believe I'm not "indwelled by the Holy Spirit." I do know that the Holy Spirit lives in me. But I'm confused about what it means to be indwelled or filled by the Holy Spirit.

A: Some denominations make a major doctrinal issue of speaking in tongues as the initial evidence of the baptism in the Holy Spirit. I believe the power of the Holy Spirit can manifest in a number of ways. But one thing can be said of speaking in tongues.

The speech centers represent the highest part of the human brain, and speech is the main characteristic that distinguishes human beings from animals. Animals can, of course, have a rudimentary type of signaling device—especially crows and dolphins—but coherent, intelligent speech is the unique characteristic of human beings. If the Holy Spirit has control of the speech centers and has given His anointing, this is clear evidence that His presence is working in the individual. I believe it is unwise to try to put an infinite God in some type of doctrinal straitjacket and claim this is the only way in which He can accomplish a particular task. We should leave our understanding open to whatever way the infinite God deals with any one of His creatures.

Q: Can I pray to the Holy Spirit?

A: If you want the technically correct form of prayer, we pray to the Father in the name of Jesus Christ His Son, and in the power of the Holy Spirit. However, I for one see no reason why a believer should not ask for help from the Holy Spirit Himself. We do have several hymns in evangelical churches such as "Sweet Holy Spirit" and "Spirit of the Living God." We feel that worship and prayer to the Holy Spirit are absolutely appropriate.

Q: Does every Christian get a spiritual gift?

A: Scripture tells us that God sends gifts to His children in accordance with His will. The Apostle Paul told believers to earnestly desire the better gifts, especially that they should prophesy. Remember that the Holy Spirit Himself is the gift. Beyond that, in His sovereign will, He makes the things of Jesus known to believers and will divide His power to His people according to His sovereign will.

Q: How can I discover my spiritual gift?

A: I believe that God makes each one of us with particular abilities and talents. We are always happiest when we do the thing that God has made us for. We should not envy others but should stir up the gift that is within us. That's what Paul wrote to Timothy—"stir up the gift of God which is in you through the laying on of my hands" (2 Timothy 1:6 NKJV). If anyone has the power of the Holy Spirit within them, He, the Spirit, will manifest Himself in a way that is appropriate.

Q: Is there a limit to how many spiritual gifts a person receives?

A: The Holy Spirit is the gift. The Holy Spirit is not limited. Imagine what He placed in this earth and imagine what His universe consists of. He is not limited, and His potential toward each one of us is not limited.

Q: Does God allow the Holy Spirit to speak to us through other people?

A: I am very cautious about directive prophecy that comes to an individual through some other Christian person. I've had people say they were bringing me messages from the Lord, and they were totally mistaken. A woman came to John Wesley and said God had told her that he was "bedding down with a whore." John answered, "The Lord knows me better than that. He didn't send you." It is so easy for some supposedly spiritual person to try to direct the course of somebody else under the guise of bringing a message from the Lord.

In the Old Testament, however, God sent prophets to warn kings about conduct that was not pleasing to Him. He also sent messengers to encourage them in a particular course of action. In my opinion, the question is the track record of the person who is bringing the message. One of the most helpful ways to receive guidance is through a confirming word from a friend or spiritual advisor as to something the Lord has already told you.

Q: Does the Holy Spirit place His power or anointing on places or things? For example, people say, "The anointing is really on that place."

A: When Solomon dedicated the Temple, the power of God came down so strongly that the priests could not stand to minister. There also seemed to be a special anointing on the Ark of the Covenant, because an individual was struck dead if he happened to lay a hand on it. We're told a dead man was dropped into the grave with Elisha and came back to life from having contact with his bones. We sing, "There's a sweet, sweet spirit in this place, and I know it is the Spirit of the Lord." From all of this, we can say the answer is yes.

Q: How do we grieve the Holy Spirit?

A: We grieve the Holy Spirit when we act directly contrary to what we know is His will, especially if He's given us guidance about a course of action and we deliberately disobey it. We grieve Him when we disobey His word. We grieve Him when we engage in sin. We grieve Him when we deny His reality.

Q: How do I know the Holy Spirit is truly speaking to me, not my imagination or something evil?

A: The Bible tells us that the mature are those who have exercised their senses so they can discern good from evil. There is no shortcut to plain old trial and error. We exercise our senses, listen to the Lord, and then try to follow what He tells us. But we gain maturity as we walk with Him and talk with Him and get His guidance confirmed in our lives.

Obviously, every impression that comes to our minds is not from the Holy Spirit. There are many spiritual voices in the world, and we must exercise our senses to discern which are good and which are bad. I should emphasize at this point that the Holy Spirit will not contradict the Word of God. If we think we have a message from the Holy Spirit which is contrary to Scripture, we know it is not from God. As the Apostle Paul said, "But even if we, or an angel from heaven, should preach to you a gospel contrary to what we have preached to you, he is to be accursed!" (Galatians 1:8 NASB).

Q: If I have resisted the Holy Spirit in the past but have repented, will He restore His promptings back into my life so that I can hear from Him?

A: Absolutely. He will, but you must go back to that place where you went astray. Face what you've done and ask God's forgiveness. I recommend sitting down with a pen and paper and writing down those areas in your life where you know you've sinned against the Lord. Confess those things to Him. Ask His forgiveness. Then take the paper and burn it up, because God wants your conscience cleansed from dead works so that you might serve Him (Hebrews 9:14). God wants us to be useful in His Kingdom, not burdened down with guilt. So of course He will restore His promptings to you if you will confess the sin that brought you the problem.

Q: I'm afraid that I have committed the unpardonable sin by rejecting the Holy Spirit. Have I lost my salvation?

A: As a young Christian, I was living in the joy of the Lord because I had a whole new life. Once, after I had been praying, a thought came to me that I now recognize was from the enemy: *This is nothing but a trick. You think you've been saved and are part of the fellowship of God, but you have committed the unpardonable sin, and you will never be forgiven.*

I was crestfallen. My fledgling Christian life was crashing about me. What could I do? In my prayer, a clear word burst forth from my lips: "Lord Jesus, I believe in You, and even if I'm in Hell, I will still praise You as my Savior." Then the terrible sense of grief left me, and I realized that I had not committed any unpardonable sin. The enemy of my soul was taking this one scripture and using it to destroy me. But happily, God had other plans.

In the Greek language, the *aorist* tense of a verb conveys a one-time action, and the present tense is continuing action. The word about the sin against the Holy Spirit is in the *aorist* tense—one time only. But if this is the case, it goes against everything else we are taught in the Bible. I believe, on the one hand, that the true meaning of the unpardonable sin is to attribute the work of the Holy Spirit to Satan. But the other and more profound unpardonable sin is this: refusing to repent of sin and yield to the wooing of the Holy Spirit as He leads us to faith in Jesus Christ. If we refuse to listen to the voice of the Holy Spirit and believe that Jesus Christ is the Son of God who died for our sins and rose again, then there is no forgiveness. This to me is the unpardonable sin—not a careless remark that some youngster makes before he or she finds the Lord.